CARMELITE MONASTERY

W9-CLJ-655

ᑎNT

MORAL DILEMMAS

BY THE SAME AUTHOR

THE DIVINE PITY
THE EAGLE'S WORD
THE HIGH GREEN HILL
THE PARADISE TREE
THE SEVEN SWORDS
THE SON'S COURSE
THE WATER AND THE FIRE
MORALS AND MAN
ST THOMAS AQUINAS
TO HEAVEN WITH DIANA!
THE HEART OF MAN
ON BEING HUMAN
MORALS MAKYTH MAN
MORALITY AND WAR
OF HIS FULLNESS
HIS WILL IS OUR PEACE
EVE AND THE GRYPHON
THE PAIN OF CHRIST
AWAKEN HEAVEN
THE TWO TREES

with P. K. Meagher, O.P.

STONES OR BREAD?

MORAL DILEMMAS

GERALD VANN, O.P.

1965

DOUBLEDAY & COMPANY, INC., GARDEN CITY, NEW YORK

NIHIL OBSTAT
JOANNES M. T. BARTON S.T.D. L.S.S.
CENSOR DEPUTATUS
IMPRIMATUR
PATRITIUS CASEY VIC. GEN.
WESTMONASTERII, DIE 27 JULII 1964

The Nihil Obstat and Imprimatur are a declaration that a book or pamphlet is considered to be free from doctrinal or moral error. It is not implied that those who have granted the Nihil Obstat and Imprimatur agree with the contents, opinions or statements expressed

241
Vm

Library of Congress Catalog Card Number 65–24685
Copyright © 1965 by Mark Brocklehurst
All Rights Reserved
Printed in the United States of America

ACKNOWLEDGEMENTS

Acknowledgement is due to the following for permission to incorporate here material previously published : to the editor of *Blackfriars* for chapters 5–7, 10–12, 14–15; to the editors of *Spiritual Life* (U.S.A.) and *Homiletic and Pastoral Review* (U.S.A.) for chapters 2 and 8 respectively; to the editor of the *Clergy Review* for chapters 12 and 15; and to Messrs. Burns, Oates and Washbourne for chapter 4 (from *Springs of Morality*); to the Guild of Pastoral Psychology for chapter 1. Chapters 3, 9, and 13 have not been previously published.

The publishers would also like to thank the following for permission to use quotations : The Mercier Press for *New Problems in Medical Ethics*; Messrs. Sheed & Ward for quotations from *Psychoanalysis and Personality* by Fr. Joseph Nuttin; Methuen & Co. for *Moral Values in the Ancient World* by J. Ferguson; Faber & Faber for *Passion and Society* by D. de Rougement; Longmans, Green & Co. for *The Pattern of Love* by William Wylie; Burns, Oates & Washbourne for *The Enemies of Love* by Dom Aelred Watkin; T. & T. Clark for *I and Thou* by M. Buber; Meridian Books Inc. for *Witchcraft* by Charles Williams; Constable & Co. for *The Wandering Scholars* by H. Waddell.

CONTENTS

CONTENTS

PUBLISHER'S NOTE

The author made the selection for this book before his death in July 1963. He had intended to do further work on it, and to write an introduction, but was sadly unable to carry this through. In a book made up as this one is from a variety of articles and papers on certain main themes, some repetition is inevitable. But it was clearly undesirable for us to start tampering with chapters that stand as complete units, and we have merely referred the reader to similar passages that occur elsewhere.

1. MISUNDERSTOOD MORALITY

It struck me the other day that perhaps one should write a book entitled *Alleluia*, and subtitled, of course, *I'm a Bum* : a young man back from a job in the U.S.A. had asked my advice—he was torn between wanting to marry (which would mean getting a settled job, a steady income) and wanting to be free and feckless and, as they say over there, to bum around and see the world. I suggested that for him this should not be an either-or problem, since both desires lay deep in him, but one of integration : the business-man, the family man, must accept and love the bum, must try to give him his innings but within the framework of a unified life-pattern, and therefore must make friends with him so as to be able to discuss things with him at need in a reasonable way : a good thing, I added, to give him a name—and the obvious name, it then occurred to me, was Alleluia ; finally, I said, he must marry a girl who would love and accept both sides of his personality and so help him to achieve his integrity.

All this is by way of parable. The tension (so common to-day) between constricting economic routine or social convention and the desire to make one's own life in one's own way is often paralleled in the sphere of morality by a conflict between standards imposed from without and one's own inner drives, desires or convictions.

We are to deal here with misunderstood morality ; our main concern then will doubtless be with conflicts arising from the fact that moral standards are regarded as something purely arbitrary, conventions (which usually in practice means conventional taboos, fettering restrictions and prohibitions) imposed by society, by ecclesiastical authority or by some remote deity, without any reference to right reason or the nature and needs of the individual. But it may be helpful if, to clear the ground, we consider first the sort of conflict that confronts a man who has accepted a moral code, intellectually, as valid and reasonable, yet finds that what is thus his own personal ethic is opposed by something else within him, that his will or his desires run counter to his mind.

In most if not all of us there is an antinomian, a moral Alleluia who has only to see a notice saying 'Keep off the grass' to be filled with an obsessive urge to step on the grass; 'compulsory reading' can seldom seem compulsorily readable; but also in most if not all of us there are urges which, law or no law, we know to be ugly, dark, destructive, evil, a character for whom Alleluia ceases to be an appropriate name—Miserere might do better. Let us then leave Alleluia for the moment; and consider this darker character. The problem remains one of integration: repression will lead to disaster, but so also will the policy of simply giving Miserere his head, giving him *carte blanche*, since moral amorphousness, the lack of any coherent moral attitude, can hardly be expected to produce harmony or integrity of the personality. What then can be done? How can evil be assimilated without destroying good?

Dr. Jung, while admitting that 'a unification of opposites can only be *thought* of as their destruction,'[1] makes a distinction between perfection (or perfect goodness) and completeness (or the unification of good and evil) in favour of the latter: to be psychologically complete the Christian image of the Trinity must, he argues, be turned into a quaternity by inclusion of the devil; a symbol of this completeness being the crucified Christ hanging between the two thieves. Here, I confess, I become thoroughly muddled and unable to follow: whatever else

[1] Dr. Bach thus underlines 'thought' in quoting the sentence in his lecture on *Aion* (Guild of Pastoral Psychology Lecture no. 74).

it may be, this last symbol is surely dynamic, concerned with process, not with completion: the moment is a climax indeed, but not a conclusion; in Aristotelean terms it is *energeia*, not *entelecheia*; but it is precisely entelechy that completeness seems to involve: a coming to the *telos*, the end, the consummation, which is also in some sense a coming to rest, as we say of a symphony that after building up to its climax the music comes to rest in the resolution of its final chord. In Hebrew idiom, totality is expressed by a conjunction of opposites, so that, for instance, the tree of the knowledge of good and evil could mean the tree of omniscience—a fact of which the serpent took advantage—but, nonetheless, in the same book of *Genesis*, evil is depicted as an animal at the door, crouching to spring, and Cain was told: 'It shall lust after thee, but thou canst have the mastery over it' (cf. *Gen.* iv, 7). Mastery is not mere conjunction: it may imply inclusion, incorporation, but only after a transforming process has been carried out, as animals are included in the home when they have been domesticated. Similarly, synthesis is not merely a conjunction of thesis and atithesis: it is a 'new creature,' born of the resolution of the tension between the two terms by the transforming of the two terms. If completeness is integration or integrity, integrity in its turn is purity in the original sense of the term *purus*, free of any admixture of base alloy, as we speak still of pure gold or pure nonsense. Dr. Zimmer, in his lecture on *Integrating the Evil*[2], spoke of a 'plenitude acquired through the integration, in a reconcilable form, of [evil's] own black essence': the operative word is clearly 'reconcilable,' and reconciliation implies not a simple conjunction (like the joining in matrimony of Socrates and Xantippe), but a transformation. That surely is the alchemy of redemption, productive of an integrity which is at once both wholeness and holiness.

Admittedly, words like perfection or holiness are rather

[2] Guild of Pastoral Psychology Lecture no. 39.

frightening: nice people, we find, are always much nicer if they are also rather naughty; but this seems to be true only if we take the word naughty in its modern, not its archaic sense: imperfections in a fine personality are lovable in the same sort of way as imperfections in a hand-made as opposed to a machine-made artefact, and they are not incompatible with holiness; but there is nothing lovable about stark evil, about malice, cruelty, envy, hate.

What then can reconcile *real* evil? I cannot think the answer lies in a simple *pecca fortiter*, partly because evil is of its nature disintegrating (as in the picture of Dorian Gray), partly because to abandon oneself to sin is, in St. Paul's phrase, a bondage, and partly also because an apparently humble acquiescence in one's squalor can so easily be or become in fact a form of pride, an inverted perfectionism, a *pharisaïsme du publicain*, a cult of degradation. Nor can I think Dr. Zimmer's statement, that 'only a sinner can become a saint', quite accurate: there are 'child-saints' (whatever their age by the calendar) whose lives are songs of innocence; though certainly it is often through sin-repented that sanctity is born, and there is truth in the remark made by Mrs. Christopher in Miss Elizabeth Myers' novel of that name, that 'sinners are the ones who best understand love because sin asks for love, calls it out and creates it more poignantly than anything else on earth.'

In fact, the vast majority of us have no need to go in search of sin: we are sinful enough and to spare already, and well aware of the fact. (The innocent need to be 'made sin' for the sake of their brethren, for we cannot help where we do not understand, with that deep understanding we call sympathy, but to be 'made sin' as Christ was, not by sinning but by knowing, suffering, the nature, the malice and the pain, of sin.) No, the clue to the reconciling of our sin surely lies in the word 'love', with its ambivalence of tenderness and sternness. When we say to someone 'I love you,' the 'you' must, if we are speaking truth, be not a fantasy-figure, an idealization; it must be this human being which confronts us, compounded of good qualities and of bad; but loving a whole personality does not imply an uncritical approval of everything in the personality: it is a will-to-good, *ti voglio bene*, and implies therefore a fierce desire to help in remedying, redeeming, what is evil. It is the same with ourselves: we are to accept and love whatever is there, darkness and light, evil and good, together: but that means, not acquiescing in the evil, but longing for the redemption of the evil, longing for the darkness to become light, the water to be turned into wine. And that transubstantiation is possible because the raw material out of which evil is fashioned is also potentially the raw material of good: the 'slime of the earth', the potter's clay, can become either a thing of beauty or a repulsive mess.

At this point we meet a common but disastrous misunderstanding, which Dr. Jung himself seems to share: a misreading of the old definition of evil as *privatio boni*. This is interpreted as meaning that evil is a mere absence of good, having no reality, no real existence, of its own; which of course is nonsense, and makes nonsense both of Christ's personal *agon* and of the basic Christian idea of life in this world as a ceaseless warfare against an all too real and substantial enemy, against the might of that mystery of iniquity of which St. Paul speaks. *Privation* has in fact been confused with *negation*: which is to equate the sightlessness of a stone with the sightlessness of Samson, or being unformed (which can be very lovely, like the promise of spring, or Lolita), with being deformed (which is ugliness). There is a further confusion between the merely material and the formal or significant aspects of a situation: it makes no significant difference whether a deformity is due to excess or defect of matter —you can ruin a beautiful statue either by hacking chunks out of it or by slapping chunks on to it; elephantiasis and shrunken limbs are both signs of a defective physique, both deformities or privations. Moral deformity, too, is a twisting or wrenching of something 'out of true' and therefore out of the natural (or supernatural) goodness and beauty it ought to have. The same physical action can express either love or hate; and of course both are real : the hatred has reality, a horrible and hideous reality; but if it occurs in a situation which of its nature ought to be love-filled (as, for instance, a brutally or contemptuously loveless act of sexual intercourse), then essentially the situation is deformed by being wrenched out of love, and the evil *is* this. deformity in it.

Now the main significance of all this is that though evil, in this view, is indeed a reality, and a vast and terrifying reality, still it is not an ultimate; it is, so to speak, housed in goodness, it is a corruption of what is good. Satan is still Lucifer, though his beauty is ravaged and twisted, he has wrecked his integrity. (Incidentally, it is surely not, as Dr. Jung maintains, the image of Christ which is incomplete because it excludes the darkness, but Satan who is incomplete, mutilated, because he cut himself off from the light; so, in popular legend, it is he, the devil, who is supposed to cast no shadow : how could he, since he is not 'in the light', he is himself—morally speaking— all shadow.) Man's beauty, too, is ravaged; he is maimed and twisted; but he is not wholly evil; and the same energies which can be thrown into deeds of darkness can also be put to the 'service of the Light'. Ruthless aggressiveness or the heroic fortitude that conquers dizzy heights; tyranny and the lust for domination or a creative, beneficent use of administrative genius; orgiastic sensual depravity or the power and poetry of that lyrical passion that stirs the heart of the world; the will-to-death which is the grin of despair or the will-to-life-through-death which is the smile of humble hope, reflecting and evoked by that other Smile of the *luce eterna che ami ed arridi*— each of these pairs are like opposite sides of a coin : the same metal, a different imprint, a different seal.

To the question then of how evil is to be reconciled, we can now offer a double answer : (1) We can try to di-

vert the energies which have been put to destructive uses
into new, creative channels; (2) We can accept the evil
that has been done and the seal it has set on us, not as
something to be fled or forgotten, not as an occasion for
remorse (which is itself sterile and destructive), but as
an occasion for creative sorrow, for that *metanoia*, that
change of mind and heart, which is a darkness productive
of light, a death productive of life, because out of the
sorrow love is born, and love begets life. And perhaps this
second thing helps one to achieve the first, since it is into
a *deeper* life and light that one is thus reborn; for sin,
though not entirely to be explained by ignorance as Socrates held, is often in great measure due to it, and to be
superficial *is* to be ignorant. The man who is intellectually
convinced of the rightness of monogamy, but whose
drives and urges make him polygamous, promiscuous, is
more likely to be able to redeem his drives once sorrow
has made him aware of the 'tragic sense of life', the tragedy and pathos of human creatures who, if one treats
them Herrick-like as rosebuds to be wantonly plucked
and discarded, become lay-figures and elude one, so that
life eludes one, too. One deep volition can control many
velleities; a deep love will dominate and redeem many
amourettes. That is not to say that the diversion of energies from destructive to creative uses is always easy, or
even always possible : it is part of the untidiness of our
fallen world that what is desirable and beneficial at one
level may not seem so, or even be so, at another; physiological, psychological, moral do not always chime together.

Now we find this untidiness and complexity greatly
increased when we turn to the second, the main, type of
tension we have to consider, where moral laws are regarded simply as arbitrary conventions, unsupported by
reason, unconnected with the nature of reality. Here indeed we may have a triangle drama : first, the instinctive
drives at war with the conventions, and often victorious,
yet finding perhaps that victory leaves a sour taste, a

mysterious, because irrational and inexplicable, guilt-sense; and then drives and conventions alike opposed by some sort of personal ethic, perhaps simultaneously sincere yet ill-conceived, whence further conflicts.

The psychotherapist is trained never to pass moral judgment on his patient: the moment he begins to 'look shocked' or to moralize, to sermonize, his power to help is at an end. Yet he is always finding himself faced with troubles which are due to moral conflicts, and often I suppose the root cause will in fact be the lack (the priva-tion, not negation) of a coherent, intellectually and per-sonally satisfying, moral attitude. In such cases he cannot try to impose on the patient his own ethical code; but he can help him to examine for himself what he has *assumed* to be ethical imperatives, and to separate wheat from chaff, intellectually valid principles from valueless and perhaps harmful conventionalities, in order to build up for himself a coherent and convincing moral theory.

When the ordinary man nowadays talks of conven-tional morality he probably means a muddled amalgam of the purely conventional behaviour-patterns (what is and is not 'done') of his social group, with some residual tags from the Christian ethic which, as like as not, have been distorted either by sentimentalization or by being wrenched from their setting in the Christian *Weltan-schauung* and thus robbed of their *rationale*. It may then be helpful simply to point out to him certain *facts* about the Christian ethic, as material for a personal judgment.

First, this ethic comprises basic principles of conduct which are not confined to Christianity or Judaeo-Chris-tianity, but are in effect universal: these are called the 'natural law', as being consonant with and determined by the nature of man, and indeed of reality as a whole as we know it: and 'consonant with the nature of man' in its turn means both consonant with reason (for man is by nature a reason-using animal), and also describing man's way to the fulfilment of his nature, to perfection and (*pace* Dr. Jung) completeness. That the basic princi-

ples common to Christian and pagan alike do in fact describe such a pattern is perhaps most easily demonstrated
by the undeniably dire effects of a consistent repudiation
of them: Dorian Gray is again relevant, as is St. Paul's
notion of the 'bondage of sin' as against the 'freedom of
the sons of God'. Thus far, then, Christianity and humanism march together; and love of the law rightly understood *is* love of life.

But, secondly, it can be dangerous to speak of a moral
law at all, inasmuch as the word 'law' is used in so many
different senses, from the laws of physics or dynamics
which simply describe how and why things happen as
they do, to the civil laws which prescribe how things shall
be done and which are often arbitrary and sometimes
stupid or unjust. For the Christian there are indeed moral
injunctions which are binding solely because the authority of the Church has so decided (as, for instance, for
the Roman Catholic, Sunday Mass and Friday fish),
though such laws are conditional both on circumstances
(it is not a sin to miss Mass if one is ill) and on consonance
with basic moral principles (it is a sin to go to Mass if that
means abandoning one's dying mother). But where these
basic moral principles are concerned, even though they
may *de facto* be promulgated as laws in the Bible or by
the Church, still the things they forbid are forbidden
because they are wrong, they are not wrong simply because they are forbidden, and the things commanded are
commanded because they are right and not *vice versa*.

This last sentence leads to a third essential point: so far
as attitude of mind is concerned, primacy of importance
must be given to what is commanded rather than what is
forbidden: the Christian ethic as a whole is meant to lead
to wholeness and holiness: and these denote essentially
a state of being. Thus Don't is for the sake of Do, and
Do is for the sake of Be. (This is in direct contrast to the
common view of morality as an endless series of taboos.)
In the Christian view we must avoid evil because other-

wise we shall not do good; and we must do good so as
in the end to be good, to be whole.

Fourthly, we must do good, hoping thus in the end to
be good, in order to be true not only to our own nature
but to reality as a whole—for if we are in revolt from reality we are like Satan : darkness, misery, hatred. The natural law is defined as the reflection in us of the 'eternal
law' which in its turn is defined (by St. Thomas) as the
ratio—we might say the design or pattern—of divine wisdom as directive of all activities and processes : that wisdom which is the Word, expressing as it were the inner
rhythm of the Godhead and on the other hand describing
what creation does or, in free creatures, ought to do to reflect that divine reality. (So for example we ought to be
true—which means much more than just verbal veracity
—in order to reflect the beauty of God who is truth; we
ought to love, or rather be love, live in love, to reflect the
beauty of the uncreated Love.) Our concept of the moral
law thus comes closer now in one respect to that of physical laws : not arbitrary and perhaps senseless taboos, but
the rhythm or pattern of reality. And we shall expect to
find, and do find, that pattern pervading the whole tex-
ture of created reality, expressed alike in Nature and art,
in myth, in the conscious speculations of philosophers
and in the dreams and imaginative creations in which
man's unconscious is revealed.

For what is the essence of sin ? In *Genesis* the original
sin is pictured for us as the eating of a tempting apple
('fair to the eyes, and delightful to behold') in defiance
of the authority of God; in other words, as greed and pride
or ego-worship. They wanted to dethrone God and be
themselves as gods, making all things their creatures to
be used as they wished. (In fact they lost the dominion
they had originally possessed : the animals refused to
obey them, Nature became hostile to them, and even their
own personalities became disrupted, flesh rebelling against
spirit, so that they became frightened of their own bodies
as they had become frightened of their God, hiding the

one as they hid from the other.) And the only way to redeem the situation, to recover wholeness, harmony, the proper dignity and stature of man, lies through a humble acceptance of the Other. All the principal forms of wrongdoing are in fact reductively expressions of ego-worship and greed: the lust for power, dominance, autonomy; the lust for pleasure, the lust to possess; and the ten commandments, which express the principles of the natural law, counter these lusts by the acceptance of heteronomy: of the rights and claims upon us, first of the Creator, then of man, the human family, our neighbour, and then finally of our own human nature, the psychophysical entity which is (or is to become) the Self. When Harriet Martineau said 'I accept the universe,' Carlyle commented 'By God, she better had!'—but her words can be taken as expressing a profound and not always recognised truth about human life. When Huxley said that the scientist must sit down before the facts like a child, he was echoing a much wider and deeper injunction: Christ told us, not that we must *be* children—on the contrary, we have to grow up, become mature, become wise —but that we must *become again* as little children, be born again by accepting what is greater than ourselves, learning, labouring, not so much to possess truth or love or to capture joy as to be possessed by truth and love and to enter into joy.

But this reversal is possible only through darkness, the rebirth is possible only through death; and this pattern of life-through-death is writ large for us throughout reality. Moreover, it is made plain that this is something we cannot simply do for ourselves but that must be done in us: St. Paul's 'Not that, left to ourselves, we are able to frame any thought as coming from ourselves; all our ability comes from God',[3] or the 'He that is mighty hath done great things in me' of the *Magnificat*. The waters that are above must come down and bedew the earth if the waters

[3] II *Cor.* iii, 5.

below are to spring up into life; and for that a hole must be made in the firmament by a pillar or pole or tree rising up into the sky : but the pillar must be sacred, consecrated and blessed, the tree must be God's tree, Christ's tree, God-given and given to God, like the stone set up and anointed by Jacob in the place which was filled with awe because of the Presence in it, and which therefore he called the house of God and the gate of heaven. (The Babel-ziggurat, on the other hand, could not reach to the sky because it was man-made, man-reliant, and so it ended in disaster, the wreckage of human solidarity, the enmity born of fear, born of incomprehension which springs up between people or peoples who have nothing in common, who do not 'speak the same language'.) The same theme recurs endlessly, inside and outside the Bible, from great poetry or myth down to the humble nursery-rhyme or an apparently frivolous fantasy like Humpty-Dumpty.

Humpty-Dumpty sat on a wall—

the ovoid figure (reminiscent of the birth of certain he-roes of mythology) with tiny, wholly inadequate legs, sitting on (perhaps) a garden-wall, the wall of the 'garden enclosed', the garden of Eden (the word 'paradise' means an enclosed park), and feeling that the garden, for all its beauty, was not enough for him, the wall (like the broad belt that Tenniell gave him) restricted him : he wanted new worlds to conquer—and the accent is on the conquering : in the garden he was not his own master and he wanted to be himself a king—but his dwarf-like lower limbs let him down, he 'had a great fall' which broke him into pieces (so also Jack in the nursery-rhyme, Jill's friend, having tried to climb the hill and fetch the pail of water 'as of himself', fell down and broke his crown —where 'crown' has the nice ambiguity of suggesting both cranium and regal diadem); and Humpty-Dumpty's dream of kingly glory thus came to an abrupt end—he broke up and woke up—and he found that neither the would-be king's horses (his animal energies) nor his men (his rational nature) could put him together again, could re-integrate him. What Humpty should have done was ride acock-horse to Banbury Cross: according to the OED, one of the meanings of 'acock' is 'defiantly': defiance, here, perhaps of the wiles of Satan, perhaps of any bogies of timidity of his own which might tempt him to turn back to the safety of the womb, or perhaps, most important in the context, defiance of his own megalomaniac dreams of kingship, his own pride, which would make him repudiate the folly of the cross. Doubtless, too, his horse should be not a magnificent white charger but the little shaggy horse of the Celtic myth of Conn-eda, which seems much closer to the donkey on which Abraham rode to the mount of vision to surrender his son Isaac, his Laughter, or on which the boy David rode to the camp of Saul to do battle with the giant, or again on which Christ, the king-victim, shepherd and lamb, judge and man of sorrows, rode into Jerusalem, on his way to Calvary Cross.

The idea of Humpty scurrying back to the safety of the womb, retreating from life, in direct contrast to the symbol of the heroic and perilous return to the womb to be reborn and start life afresh, suggests a reflection on the various forms of sin by defect, of life-refusal: cowardice, timidity, small-mindedness, meekness and mildness misinterpreted as lack of spirit, humility misinterpreted as craven obsequiousness, prudence misinterpreted as always playing for safety, and so on. One tends to think of ego-worship in terms of grandiosity, megalomania; but these refusals, too, are fundamentally forms of ego-worship because forms of ego-coddling: I am so precious, I must be wrapped up in cotton-wool, I must not be exposed to the violence of wind and rain, of thunder and tempest, nor, for that matter, to the dangerous rough-and-tumble of life among the vulgar.

There is a very interesting and striking contrast between a passage of *Isaiah* in which God is speaking to

mankind and an old Catalonian legend[4] about a little
tom-thumb personage called Padre Patufet. In the first,
God says to man: 'My thoughts are not your thoughts,
nor your ways my ways. . . . For as the heavens are
exalted above the earth, so are my ways exalted above
your ways, and my thoughts above your thoughts. And
as the *rain and snow come down from heaven,*[5] and return no more thither, but soak the earth, and water it,
and make it to spring, and give seed to the sower, and
bread to the eater: so shall my word be.' In the Catalonian legend, Patufet is so tiny that one day he gets lost
in the country, and a kindly ox swallows him to protect
him; while he is thus in the belly of the ox he hears his
parents calling to him, 'Where are you?' and he replies,
'I am in the belly of the ox where *it does not snow and it
does not rain.*' Patufet, or Jonah (or of course him whose
sojourn in the tomb Jonah's story foreshadowed): the
refusal or the acceptance of the challenge of life, of reality; the will to death or the will to life through death:
we have to choose. And if we want life, if we want reality,
then we have to have the snow and the rain from heaven,
we have to go out of doors and get uncomfortably wet;
only then shall we have seed for our sowing and bread
for our eating.

Now if we can thus see moral principles as pointing the
way to life, to complete vitality and integrity, we certainly shall not think of them as pointless conventions;
neither shall we see them simply in terms of a prescribed
code, weighing down on us from without. (And here we
come back to Alleluia or Miserere, to the antinomian in
us: we have at least something now to offer him by way
of pacification, for to the antinomian the law, the *nomos*,
loses a great deal of its sting when it is seen as coming
under the heading of what, in Greek thought, stands in
direct contrast to *nomos*, namely *physis*, nature.) We

---

[4] Mentioned in *The Secret Life of Salvador Dali.*
[5] Italics mine.

cannot escape from the bondage of the law by a repudiation of the law, an amorphous hedonism, which leads
only to disintegration and to the bondage of sin; the law
is bondage so long as we feel it as something external to
us and imposed on us : we escape the bondage by making
it *internal*, an expression not of some alien will but of our
own. And this is the first way of internalizing it : to see it
in terms of *physis*, the pattern of our own growth to
completeness, to that holiness which, far from excluding,
essentially includes humanness and the positive values
of humanism.

But though we may be able to see the broad outlines
of the Christian ethic in this light, we may not be able,
because of the untidiness of our fallen world, to see some
particular moral principle as it bears on a particular situation in the same light. Here a second note of internaliza-
tion may be possible. If we have seen with our minds and
felt with our hearts the meaningfulness of creative darkness, we may be able to see this very untidiness, and the
at least apparently insoluble problems to which it gives
rise, as part of that darkness. This, however, requires not
only great strength, maturity, wisdom, but also a profound humility; here, therefore, the importance of the
child-symbol so stressed by Christ and so constantly re-
current in the Bible and elsewhere is particularly obvious.
Again and again in the Bible-story worldly wisdom is re-
jected in favour of the child; again and again, as St. Paul
saw so clearly, God turns the wisdom of the world to
folly, for 'the foolishness of God is wiser than men, and
the weakness of God is stronger than men' and 'the
foolish things of the world hath God chosen, that he may
confound the wise; and the weak things of the world
hath God chosen, that he may confound the strong'—and
why all this? In order, St. Paul says, that 'no flesh should
glory' in God's sight[6] : the *rationale* of the rationally insoluble is our need of rebirth and therefore our need of

[6] cf. I *Cor.* i, 20–9.

learning to be humble. (And, since donkeys have been mentioned, we might reinforce this lesson by recalling the story of Balaam, whom neither learning nor experience nor even his prophetic powers could save from folly, so that he needed the help of a poor dumb animal to teach him a little horse-sense.)

But there is a third way of internalizing the law, and it is the most important of all because it is all-embracing. We can express it in popular language in the words of the old adage : Love me, love my dog. We all know how, if asked to do something by someone we dislike, we probably either refuse or else do it with an ill grace ; if asked to do the same thing by someone we love, we probably do it with alacrity. If we fall in love with the Lawgiver, we must in the end come to love his law because it is his will for us. And so our own will may lovingly accept what otherwise it would reject as intolerable, just as the mind may accept with childlike trust what otherwise it would repudiate as folly.[7]

Yet even as in some deeply loved vocation (of art, of music, of marriage) there must be dark, arid periods when its routine, its drudgery, its demand for protracted effort become intolerable and the life itself seems a captivity from which one yearns to escape, so it must be with the law of God, the pattern of life, however, clearly apprehended and deeply loved. Even St. Paul, for all his fire, found that to will the good is not necessarily to do it, and that though he 'delighted' in the law of God, he found within him another law which fought against it and repudiated it.[8] We tire so quickly, grow bored so easily, are so swift to find that any pattern, however delightful, grows irksome if it is repetitious or if its execution demands prolonged effort ; and then once again the

---

[7] The Hebrew prophets, whose concern for morality was caused by their zeal for religion, saw sin as essentially not transgression but rebellion—a fact often unfortunately obscured in translation.

[8] *Rom.* vii, 18–23.

antinomian Alleluia raises a plaintive whimper. Is there
at that point anything further that we can do? Certainly
it seems true that bread alone will not keep us quiet without occasional circuses, that there is an element of sound
sense therefore in the principle of the occasional Satur-
nalia (and the Church seems to accept this principle, in
considerably more sober form, in its alternation of feasts
and fasts, its acceptance of the pre-lenten Carnival):
we all need at times to relax and let down our hair when
effort has exhausted us, to interrupt or vary a routine
that has become took irksomely boring. But can we find a
moral justification for interrupting the routine of the
moral life? If that means even a temporary repudiation,
taking a temporary holiday from the ten commandments,
no, alas, we cannot; but repudiation is not the only way
of diversifying a routine. There is another way, and consideration of it throws further light on the nature of
morality itself and may avert thereby a further misunderstanding which we ought to have in mind. Alleluia becomes restive when the moral life seems too prosaic: but
it is one of the most salient features of Christian morality
in its fullness that it is not only prose but poetry.

Christ 'spoke in parables to the multitudes: and without parables he did not speak to them': parable is one
of the forms of symbol, of picture-language, of the poetic
as opposed to the prose or rational scientific, use of words;
and between these two uses there are two main differences, first, that, as Dr. Austin Farrer points out, the purpose of scientific language is to exclude ambiguity, the
purpose of symbol to include it; secondly, the scientific
formula appeals to the mind, the poem appeals not only
to the mind but to the heart (to intuition and in a deep
sense to feeling) as well; so the two disciples in the
Emmaus story asked, 'Did not our hearts burn within us
when he talked with us by the way?' We speak of mastering a science, but not of mastering a great poem; for
a poem is not something we can grasp and absorb by reason (we cannot paraphrase a poem, as examiners so

often demand, without destroying it), it is a mystery into which we enter; and in the radiant darkness, in the paradox, of mystery the heart discovers things that reason could never formulate. Christ taught the multitudes in paradox, sometimes clothed in parable, sometimes overt, because what he had to teach, to communicate, was the mystery of the kingdom. *Omnia abeunt in mysterium* : in the last resort all reality is, for us, mystery, paradox; and as this is true of our approach to the divine reality, the *mysterium tremendum* (as when, for instance, we say not merely that God is both just and merciful, but that his justice *is* his mercy), so it is true also of our human situation, the *chiaroscuro* in which we live. For any adequate statement of the Christian faith, doctrinal formulas are essential (as the more bizarre pages in the history of mysticism or religious enthusiasm sufficiently show), but they need to be complemented— and vitalized—by communication-through-symbol; so also both in describing and in living out the moral pattern, prose and poetry are alike essential. There are the reasoned and reasonable rules of virtuous conduct, but there is also the wind that bloweth where it listeth, that divine impulse, not irrational but suprarational, described by theology in terms of the gifts and fruits of the Spirit, giving to the lives of holy people their lyrical freshness, spontaneity, unpredictability and the apparent fecklessness and folly which prove in the end so divinely right and wise, and so causing them to stand out in such dramatic contrast to the dull (and perhaps smug) prosaic correctitude of the conventionally 'good'. Christ was not 'respectable'.

Was not Judas right when he condemned the waste of the precious ointment and spoke of the needs of the poor? Was not the prodigal son's elder brother justified in grumbling against his father's prodigality to the wastrel and ingratitude towards himself? Is it fair that heaven should rejoice over the one repentant sinner more than the ninety-nine just, that the harlots and sinners should be the first to enter the kingdom, that all the labourers in the vineyard, late comers and early alike, should receive every man a penny, that immediate paradise should be promised not to the good and faithful servants, but to a thief? The answer lies in such sayings as 'Many sins are forgiven her because she hath loved much': God is love, and therefore the essential fulfilment of the law consists in becoming love; the love does indeed imply the will to do Love's will, but it cannot be measured simply in terms of success, efficiency, in accomplishing that will. The gospels draw a vivid contrast between the 'good, respectable' people, the rule-keepers, who did not find favour with God and the 'sinners', the rule-breakers, who did; when Mrs. Christopher, in the book already referred to, remarks that at the end 'it's not what we've done that will matter—but what we'd like to have done', she is in fact echoing the *Cloud of Unknowing* : 'Not what thou art or what thou hast been, seeth God with his merciful eyes, but what thou wouldst be.' Nurse Cavell's words concerning patriotism can be applied to any moral virtue : justice is not enough, prudence is not enough : if virtue is not to be prosaic it must be transfigured by the mighty wind and fire of the Spirit of Love; whereas it can truly be said that love is enough : for if, loving God, we really will to do his will, we need not despair if we fail in accomplishment.

The 'fruits' or effects of the indwelling Spirit, listed for us by St. Paul : love, joy, peace, patience and the rest, describe the truly Christian personality, and they are essentially qualities of soul, not just a list of 'good works' (though the qualities of soul of course express themselves in outward behaviour). With love as the ultimate source of them all, these qualities follow a more or less logical order, one leading on to the next : if this love fills you and you are living in this love, you will have in you the sort of joy that is independent of circumstances and unquenched by sorrow and pain; if you have that you will be at peace, despite much turmoil and distress, and that peace will make you patient, and patience enables you to take the long view, not to clamour for slick results or quick rewards, but to keep your eyes on the distant hills, on ultimate values and ultimate ends, and so to be long-suffering in the face of difficulty or adversity. And all these qualities determine your 'social' attitudes : they make you strong enough to be always gentle, and always not just kindly but kind ; and they give you that goodness and faithfulness which are the qualities we value in a friend, the sterling, solid dependability of good wood or good workmanship and the dogged fidelity which never lets one down. All these are qualities of soul, but we are psychophysical beings, and the last fruits describe the effect on the total personality of all these qualities in terms of chastity and self-control—not just a negative absence of the disorders of sensuality, but that positive harmony and radiance which illustrate St. Thomas's definition of beauty as *splendor formae* and which are in effect a partial recovery of that harmony and integrity which, in the Christian view of things, was lost to us by the Fall, by the disintegration which followed on the primal act of ego-worship.

This is the last and perhaps greatest misunderstanding of morality : to think of it exclusively in terms of objective rules and to forget that what ultimately matters most is what is in the heart, in other words to confuse the right with the good. 'Hell,' Bernanos said, 'is not to love any more.' Love is what makes the difference between 'sinners' and sinners. Legalism (which is perhaps partly a fruit of our general hypertrophy of reason as against intuition and feeling) can cause many unnecessary sorrows, inner conflicts, perhaps despair. Too often Christians have no idea of hierarchy within the moral law (minor principles being applicable, and therefore obligatory, only in function of the major principles) and think of all laws, even purely positive laws, as wholly unconditional, so that any breakage of the rules, even though innocent or perhaps mandatory, is regarded as sinful;

external conformity is the one criterion of success in the moral life, and therefore the one thing that determines one's future destination. A Russian, Staretz, said, 'Keep thy mind in hell, and despair not': complacent rectitude is always solemn, perhaps partly from fear that if it smiles it may lose its balance; the sinner knows his own darkness, but knows also that the Light shines in the darkness and makes sin and sorrow the material of love and joy and splendour—he can laugh because he is care-free, he can cry exultantly 'Alleluia' because all the world is his to enjoy; having surrendered himself to the Wind and the Fire, he has within him the love and the joy that are independent of circumstances, even of his own sinfulness; he has conquered his ego-worship by keeping his mind in hell, in the darkness, and so he can look confidently to the light, his heart already in heaven; he knows that this is the creative darkness and so he believes, he is humbly confident, that all is well, for he has discovered the lovely paradox that to enter into that darkness is also to enter, in the end, into the joy of his Lord.

2. HOLINESS AND HUMANNESS

Sometimes one is given the experience, humbling and inspiring, of meeting people who are not merely good but holy. There is no mistaking them : they are filled, on the one hand with a quiet but profound sense of their sinfulness (a sinfulness imperceptible to everyone else), on the other hand with a vivid, infectious joy the source of which is the divine reality inside them but which at the same time is in the most down-to-earth way human, going as it does with a quick, lively interest in, love of, sympathy for people, things, all that is going on around them. There are other people who seem to be equally sin-free, prayerful, heroic, but who yet seem to lack the essential saint-quality; and if we ask ourselves why that is, we find that the answer lies in a certain remoteness, aloofness : we never really establish contact; and though they talk or listen quite kindly we feel that their attention is only fractional—the part of them that matters most is not with us but somewhere in the clouds. (But the Christian saint is passionately in love with God and man alike.) What has gone wrong?

Perhaps we shall find an answer to that question if we consider two phenomena to be met with in modern Catholic life which might seem contradictory but in fact exist simultaneously. One is the idea that the purpose of what we call grace is simply and solely to help us to keep the ten commandments. (Let us face the fact that the word 'grace' has become jargon, and therefore a bromide : this fundamental, and catastrophic, mistake might be less common if, sometimes at least, we talked not of grace but of the gift of divine life, or even of 'supervitality' . . .) To think thus is to miss the whole point of the New Dispensation, of what our Lord means by being reborn, of all that St. Paul has to say of 'newness of life'; it is (for instance) to think of charity as almsgiving whereas it means being ablaze, incandescent, with love. We do indeed need divine help if we are to keep the commandments; but in themselves they are not specifically Christian, they are the 'natural law'; and being Christians, being 'other Christs', means immeasurably more than that.

The second phenomenon is this : there are people who seem deeply pious, devout in prayer and untiring in good works, models of rectitude and pillars of the parish, but who also seem to lack not just heroic sanctity, heroic charity, but the most ordinary, commonplace, *natural* quality of kindness—and even (what is less demanding) kindliness.

Seemingly contradictory, the two things are in fact complementary : what unites them is a negativist attitude of mind. Many today think of the Christian life as meaning, first, a certain amount of church-going, saying of prayers, pious practices, and secondly, *not* breaking the commandments, which in practice boils down to *not* breaking the sixth commandment and the commandments of the Church (at least the one concerning fish on Fridays). Hence the regular church-goer (and Friday fish-eater) who is also continent may easily presume that all must be well and so may develop a sense of conscious rectitude, that monstrosity of the 'devout life'—and any normal 'reasonable mortal beast' who has to spend a day in the company of conscious rectitude will inevitably find himself longing for the company of weak, human sinners with a little natural kindness, and humbleness, in their hearts. Further, growth in holiness may easily be taken to mean piling up more and more prayers and pious practices and becoming more and more free of any sense-entanglements; and in fact many really good people, humble as well as devout, do seem to regard this as their ideal and pursue it firmly and perhaps heroically—and so may achieve something that looks very like holiness but is in fact inhuman.

To be in love with God, to be in love with his creation : that is the Christian ideal. 'By this shall men know that you are my disciples, that you have love one for another.' St. Paul says, 'I would have you aglow with the Spirit': the word is *ferventes* in the Latin, which means, as Msgr. Knox put it, 'always on the boil'. Fr. Vincent McNabb, that great and holy Friar Preacher, used to say, 'If you don't love the world don't preach to the world: preach to yourself.' St. Francis preached to the birds. Some of the saints wept, with joy and sorrow, at the loveliness of Nature's praise of God. What has gone wrong with us ? Simply this : that to be aglow with the Spirit means to be 'a burning and a shining light', filled through and through with the Light and the Fire, whereas we tend to think of it as meaning having a brilliant blaze of light in an attic while the rest of the house is left in darkness.

We are children of our age; and our age—our modern western society—is appallingly impoverished despite all the marvels, the material and scientific advantages, of modern life because in it the human personality tends to dwindle away to a fraction of itself. Modern man, unless he is unusually lucky or enlightened, leads a vestigial, a crepuscular life. Cooped up in vast towns, remote from Nature and natural things, forced to earn a living by dull, uncreative work, often sick in body or mind or both, thinking of progress in terms of technics, of faster locomotion and improved plumbing, reading little more than the newspapers and the pulp magazines, hardly aware that the life of the mind can mean more than the acquiring of utilitarian, scientific, commercial facts, finding relaxation mostly either in unimaginative sensuality or in passive amusements : it is hardly surprising if such a society is sick, neurotic : and neurotic because uncreative, and uncreative because uncontemplative.[1] (People are often

---

[1] cf. my *The Water and the Fire*, chapter 1.

amazed to hear that etymologically the word 'school' means leisure : they have forgotten the injunction, *Vacate et videte*, Be *still* and *see*—look, listen, absorb; they have forgotten what Aristotle knew, that the mind can '*become*, in a manner, all things', and they think of the educated man, not as one who has become wise through a deep and silent communion with reality, but as one with a well-stocked brain-pan.)

Christians inevitably tend to be influenced by the values of the world they live in. Consequently they tend to think of becoming a good Christian in terms of factual knowledge : knowing all the catechism answers; of faster locomotion : more and more good works and pious practices, sodalities, novenas, pilgrimages, parochial committees; and of improved plumbing : more and more devices for getting rid of vices. Hence they may miss the *unum necessarium*, the one essential thing : 'Mary hath chosen the better part' : and what was she doing ? She was doing nothing; she was neither going nor getting, she was neither acquiring factual knowledge nor engaged in good works : she was sitting still and absorbing God.

Grace, divine life, is not at a tangent to nature; grace does not live in the attic while nature inhabits the rest of the house. Grace works in and through nature, transforming it; which means working in and through and transforming these hands and feet, this head and heart, these senses, these emotions, this thinking, this willing, this living of each moment as it comes. There will be, there must be, moments when everything is excluded except the awareness of God : when hands, feet, head, heart are concerned only with his worship : your feet take you to the altar-rails, your hands are joined in prayer or hold the paten; your ears listen to words, 'The Body of Christ'; your eyes look on the Host, your mouth receives It; your emotions (if God gives you to feel devout, for it *is* a gift, it is not the stuff of holiness or devotion, but it helps) are those of adoring love, joy, sorrow, hope; your mind tries to compass something of what is being done, your will tries to give itself to God's Will: your whole personality is thus for the moment caught up in a single act of living contemplation. But such moments must be rare: we are living our earthly lives and so must eat, drink, sleep, work, play, laugh, cry, suffer, make merry, make friends, make love, make plans, make the best of many a bad job: yet all this is meant to be not an interruption of our moments of worship but a prolongation and expression of them. So St. Paul tells us that whatever we do we should do to the glory of God: all living is to be worship. We begin a meal by invoking a blessing: it is in order that the meal, *as* a meal, as a human activity, should be holy; therefore it should be, as far as possible, *humanly* well done—good, natural food, well cooked, served with a certain dignity ('the sauce to meat is ceremony') and eaten in good company, with good talk and laughter.

Those who live close to natural things, working with them or for them or making things out of them—husbandmen, foresters, shepherds, carpenters, sailors—do much more than learn about them: they learn them; and if you learn a thing, as opposed to merely learning about it, it is much easier to make your knowledge and your love of it part of your knowledge and love of God. If you want to praise God by painting on canvas you need not paint what is called a 'holy picture'; if with words, you need not write or sing a hymn; if with music, it need not be a sacred oratorio: if you are in love with God you can paint a daffodil and it will be a holy picture, you can write a poem about trees or the sea and it will be a hymn. For through Christ our Lord, divine and human, all things are made holy, and can be the material of worship, as in the Mass the bread and wine are the material of worship, the materials out of which the Sacrifice will be made. That is what living the Church's sacramental life fully means: the hallowing of everything in us, of all that goes to make up our lives.

Each of us has his individual vocation, to be and do this or that in the world, to make this or that of our lives, and to praise and worship God thereby. But whatever our individual vocations there is one duty, one basic vocation, that we all have in common : to make the best use we can of the materials within ourselves, the personal gifts, that God has given us. We all know the parable of the talents; we do not always apply its lesson to our own lives. Human beings are never static; they are as constantly in movement as a quicksand; and it is a movement either of growth or of decay : we have to choose. But growth is not just a matter of size or extent : a man does not reach physical perfection by growing and growing in girth and stature, nor does he reach full development of mind simply by learning more and more facts, or of heart simply by loving more and more individuals. We are concerned with quality as well as quantity, with depth as well as extension.

To be physiologically alive you have to breathe in and breathe out; to be psychologically alive you have to absorb, assimilate, and then express, create; but you will not in fact create unless you love what you assimilate, unless your knowledge is love-knowledge. The artist sees beauty and falls in love with it; then he both assimilates and transmutes it, making it his own; finally, he re-creates it in his own idiom. Sublimely, the same sort of process is to be found in the story of Mary, God's Mother : she listens, hears, receives; then, treasuring up words and events she ponders over them in her heart; finally, she expresses what she has now fully understood : she makes and gives to her Son in his Passion her own com-passion.

If we human beings are to absorb reality we must in every sense of the phrase come to our senses; we shall never do it unless we learn to stop and be still, to look and listen, unless we teach ourselves to use our senses thoughtfully, deeply. And this is true not only of particular realities but of Reality : we are to come to the *invisibilia Dei* through the visible things that he has created for us to

lead us to him. That is what the Church is all the time
trying to teach us : to lead a *sacramental* life, everything
a ' sacred sign ' for us ; that is why we have to react so
strongly against the kind of artificial, urbanized, commercialized existence which so often passes for real living
in our modern world, a world of go-getting where the
tempo is so frenzied that we have no time to look and
listen and may even forget that we have any need to.

The Church knows that we need formulas, texts, catechisms, need to learn *about* divine reality, need a creed
(though even so she teaches us to *sing* our credo : even
the prose of Christianity is never prosaic) ; but it knows
also that these formulas are not sufficient, that they will
become arid and dead for us unless we continually pour
into them the new vitality of immediate experience ;
hence in our worship our attention is constantly directed
to material things, natural things, to the sacred signs, the
water, wood, wine, oil, fire, that through these things (if
only, once again, we will stop and be still, look, listen,
wonder, ponder) we may learn to be wise, learn the sorrow and joy of living, learn what we are and what we are
to become, learn ' what God is like ' and how to become
like him. The Church shows us the divine answer to the
question, Shall these dry bones live ? It shows us the
divine life, the divine mercy, coming to us as water to an
arid soil, to what is dying of thirst, as fire to what is dying
of cold, as bread to the starving, as the wine that re-
joices the heart. If we live deeply and fully the Church's
liturgy we do not thereby acquire a mass of scientific
knowledge *about* water and wood and wine, we learn, we
assimilate these things themselves and the other, deeper
reality which as symbols they both conceal and reveal :
we absorb the Mystery, and therefore live it, and therefore express it in our lives.[2]

To be receptive of God, to be obedient, responsive, to
his moulding, his transforming activity within us, to be-

----

[2] cf. my *The Water and the Fire*, and *The Paradise Tree*.

come therefore God-filled, able to say in some degree 'I live, now not I, but Christ liveth in me' : this is the essence of Christianity. That is why it was suggested earlier on that we might sometimes talk of grace as super-vitality, because its effect is to make us richly, vividly, exuberantly, divinely alive, all aglow with the Spirit. That is the difference between the saint and the pious stuffed-shirt. Whom, in the Gospel, does our Lord commend? The pagan centurion, the woman who was a sinner in the city. To whom does he promise paradise? The thief on the cross. And the heroes of his best-loved parables are the prodigal son and the good Samaritan. It is the Scribes and Pharisees, with their strict fidelity to the Law, whom he denounces. Great faith, great love, humility, sorrow : these are the things that count most : many sins, as he himself told us, are forgiven those who love much.

But, the implication is clear, the love must be deep. And though it is the love of God that is here primarily in question the same is true also of the love of man. The Church gives great honour to the relationship, the sacramental union, between husband and wife : here above all other earthly experience it is a question of a deep and life-long voyage of discovery, of not just learning about but of learning, of communion at every level of the personality. But though this relationship is unique, still in the Christian view all human relationships should have in them something of the directness and depth, the personal immediacy, the reverence and the vitality, of this. In the Mass we are called a family; it is as a family that we are to approach the altar, the communion table; the word *communio* itself signifies not just a relationship between the individual soul and Christ—that would be *unio* or at any rate *co-unio*—but our common, shared union, as a family, with Christ. Just as one of the supreme glories and consolations of Christian marriage lies in the fact that through it husband and wife go together, hand in hand, to God, so it must be in some degree in every relationship between Christians : we are meant to feel responsible

for one another and to be helped by one another. It ought
to be unthinkable that a Christian should ever, through
the neglect or heedlessness of other Christians, be lonely.

So we return to the thoughts with which we started.
We can never hope to share as we should in divine reality
unless we learn to be human. The great mystic Ruysbroeck
said very wisely, 'Be kind, be kind and you will be
saints': it is as simple, and as arduous, as that. One cannot think of any of the great lovers of God as being other
than kind to their fellow-men; but the difficulty, without
that great love, of being consistently kind, all the time,
to everyone, we know all too well from our own experience. We are unkind because we are selfish; and we are
selfish because we have never learnt love, never learnt
God. But at least we can make sure that we know what
we ought to be aiming at and praying for : that increased
vitality, that divine vitality, which will set us aflame.

Let us be quite clear : the purpose of the divine vitality
is to help us keep the commandments, *is* to help us to control our senses and emotions, *is* to keep us faithful to our
prayer and our church-going, *is* to give us energy and
zeal for good works : we never outgrow the need for
these things and we cannot side-track them : there is no
short cut. The centurion was commended not because he
was a pagan but because of the greatness of his faith : if
you have enough faith you can, and you will, move mountains, even the mountain of sloth, sensuality, selfishness.
The woman was commended not because she had been a
sinner but because of the greatness of her love : if you
have enough love you will want to do, and you will do,
the will of him you love. 'If you love me, keep my commandments': our Lord might have added, 'If you love
me enough you *will* keep my commandments.' It is in
that sense that St. Augustine says *Ama et fac quod vis*:
'Love, and then do what you will' because *if* you love
God you will want to do what he wants you to do. It is
a question of emphasis; but the emphasis is of supreme
importance : it can make all the difference between a

saint and a *bien-pensant.* You could, if you liked (heaven help you!), see the Christian moral standards simply in terms of what is correct, respectable, proper, and in a cold-bloodedly dutiful way set out to live by them; and no doubt when you died you would—in your modest, mousey way—creep straight into heaven : which is a great deal more than most of us would ever dream of hoping to do. But it would be a mousey way because it would have been your way, not the specifically Christian way : something you had achieved, not something mighty done in you by Him whose Name is holy. A mousey way because though you went straight to heaven there would be little for you to take with you : the little talent of personality still tightly wrapped up in its napkin, never grown, never 'become all things', never exploded into flame, never set on fire by the great golden Lion, the Rising Sun whom we adore. A mousey way because totally prosaic, never a breath of the Christian poetry, a flick of the Eagle's wing, a hint of John the divine, the seer, learning God on the breast of God.

It is possible to spend one's life avoiding wrong-doing, and doing the conventionally right things at the right times, but never doing anything creative, never really becoming anything, and so ending up in a sort of vacuum. Far better, certainly, to do that than to spend one's life doing evil and destructive things; but it is not the Christian ideal. We sometimes forget that there is a Christian virtue called *magnanimitas,* great-heartedness; and closely allied to it there is *magnificentia* which, if it primarily means being great-hearted about material expenditures, can by extension also mean being great-hearted, prodigal, about all forms of self-giving. The pouring out of the precious ointment on Christ's feet was a magnificent gesture : it was also, as Judas was quick to point out, a waste; and in those two contrary aspects of the one gesture you have the two opposing views of life, of the good life—and only one of them is the Christian view. Man does not live by bread alone. Traditionally we define

man as an animal endowed with the power of reasoning:
that does not mean that he can live by reason alone. Judas's argument was on the face of it reasonable: but
there are times when reason is not enough. Reason is
prose: there is need of poetry as well: need (not in
defiance of reason but over and above reason) of the
Wind that bloweth where it listeth.

'Lord, I have loved the beauty of thy house': and if
his house is primarily his temple, the Church, it is also
yourself (since according to St. Paul you are the temple
of God) and *your* house—your home and family, your
company of friends, your fatherland, your earth: and
they are yours and their beauty is yours to cherish, to feel
responsible for, to learn, to love within your love of God,
that in so doing you may become wise, great-hearted,
magnificent. It is sad and unsatisfactory for a man to become a mouse, even a church-mouse, for much of the
beauty must then necessarily pass him by, and therefore
much of the *material* of living and of loving and serving
God. We are only creatures: we cannot, like God, create
out of nothing: we need the material, the beauty of the
house.

But it is not only beauty that would pass the church-
mouse by—or that one needs to be aware of to be truly
creative in the world as it exists—it is tragedy too, the
tears and the tragedy that are at the heart of things
though for the Christian they are not the last word. The
pagan could only say, *Sunt lacrimae rerum*, the tears are
there, in everything; but the Christian adds a cry of triumph: 'God will wipe away the tears from the eyes of the
saints, and there shall no more be any mourning or
weeping or any sorrow.' He *adds* his triumphant cry: he
does not shy away from the tragedy or pretend that it is
illusion: he holds that it is not the last word only in the
sense that it must be met, faced, accepted, lived through
and so in the end transcended. And it is as much a part of
the material out of which he creates—in work, in words,
in love, in life, in worship—as is the beauty of the house

and the glory that is in it. For here we work in *chiaroscuro*, in light and darkness, joy and sorrow : it is only later on that we come, if God grants it, to the place where there is no darkness but only light, and no song but that of joy unalloyed.

'He was a burning and a shining light': so our Lord spoke of the Baptist, the precursor, the pre-Christian, the man who went 'back to Nature', living in the desert, feeding on locusts and wild honey: the man therefore who in a sense represents the natural law (his baptism was a valuable sign indeed but not a grace-giving sacrament; his advice to those who came to him was concerned with the natural law of justice) but the natural law as preparation for the New Dispensation, the law of love, the wind, the water, the fire.

We have to pray, then, to be human : to be alive, aware, contemplative, creative; to be just, prudent, brave, self-controlled; to love the beauty of God's house, to be reverent in our approach to God's handiwork and especially his human handiwork, to feel both responsibility and compassion for the corruption of that handiwork, to be kind. But we have to pray too that all this may spring from an inner fire that is not of our kindling, an inner energy that is not just a human vitality and that drives us on to a great-heartedness which makes human prudence look niggardly, a love which is far more prodigal, and more lovely, than justice, a Christ-likeness which means that something much greater than the self has taken control and speaks and acts through mind and heart and senses, so that it at least begins to be true to say 'I live, now not I, but Christ liveth in me.'

3. MEDICINE AND MORALS

'I can cure the gout or stone in some,' wrote Sir Thomas Browne, 'sooner than divinity can cure pride or avarice in others. I can cure vices by physick when they remain incurable by divinity, and they shall obey my pills when they contemn their precepts.' The lot of the moralist is a hard one. In the hands of the surgeon we are as the potter's clay for we have no science with which to oppose him even if we would, and anyway we are reduced to unconsciousness before he begins. The moralist is more vulnerable. We all like to think of ourselves as competent in this field and most of us, if we judge the moral theologian to be talking nonsense, are prepared flatly to say so. But Sir Thomas, having remarked that there are 'diseases incurable in physick' as there are 'vices incorrigible in divinity', goes on to say that 'there is no catholicon or universal remedy' but death, 'which though nauseous to queasy stomachs, yet to prepared appetites is nectar, and a pleasant potion of immortality': being himself both physician and theologian he saw no incongruity between the two sciences, was ready to accept in blind faith such religious matters as were hard to explain scientifically, and saw in death the ultimate cure of the ills of body and soul alike. Today the general feeling is different: it is often thought that doctor and theologian, far from working together and aiming at a common end, must be antagonists, the purposes and postulates of the one more or less incompatible with those of the other; this is regarded as simply a particular instance of the general divorce of religion from life; and the usual comment is, So much the worse for religion.

Some today might think it a platitude to say that the priest, as official moralist, is out of touch with the people; this seems to be especially true in the sphere of medicine and morals, and it is worth inquiring why it should be so. Elsewhere we have considered the two main streams of ethical thought, the deontological and the teleological:[1] the former holding for instance that murder is wrong simply because it is forbidden by a moral code whether expressly and perhaps arbitrarily determined by God or intuitively apprehended by man; the latter seeing the inadmissibility of murder in terms of its incompatibility with man's end, his happiness, in the best sense, and thinking of law only or mainly as the pattern of what in fact leads to that happiness. The history of Christian ethical thought is to some extent a history of the duel between these two theories : as we have seen, St. Thomas established a synthesis out of them, but his influence on immediately succeeding ages was not decisive; in the medieval universities law finally triumphed over theology; with the Reformation came the impact of antirationalism and the emergence of a more pragmatic and commercial as opposed to a more purely speculative turn of mind; Catholicism found itself forced to stand on the defensive and to concern itself primarily with the remedying of wide-spread moral laxity; and all these factors combined with an already established tendency to negativism in piety and theology to produce an outlook which was in a new sense legalist, law seen more and more not as a pattern-to-happiness but as a rigid code backed by sanctions, concerned less with that *motus ab intrinesco* which is the Aristotelean definition of life, with the vitality and wise purposiveness of the good life, the loving and choosing of the good, the achieving of ultimate destiny in the love of God, than with the *minutiae* of objective moral standards, of casuistry. This attitude pro-

[1] cf. my *Morals and Man*.

foundly modified the character of subsequent moral thinking and is with us still in some measure today.

One of the ill effects of this kind of thinking was the growth of scrupulosity: the soul harassed and confused by a multitude of prohibitions tends to become perplexed in conscience, and perplexity, and the timidity engendered by fear of breaking the rules, tend to produce scrupulosity. Now legalist theologians were committed by their basic attitude of mind to dealing with this disease not by remedying the psychological atmosphere which produced it but by inventing complex systems of casuistry whereby every case could be decided straight from a book of rules; so there arose the contending factions of laxists and rigorists and tutiorists, of probabilists and probabiliorists and æquiprobabilists, some of them condemned, others allowed but unpopular, others again much in vogue for a time, but all together producing a situation which tended to increase the disease by encouraging meticulous introspection and the categorizing of this or that type of action, isolated like a fly in amber, while laying too little stress on Aristotle's wise saying that ethics can never be an exact science.

A moralist of this type is bound to appear to the popular mind as simply a combination of lawyer, diagnostician and policeman. But now another factor has to be considered: the widening gap, from the fourteenth century onwards, between theology and science. This, as we have seen, was due in part to an inner decay in the theological thinking of the time: scholasticism suffered from a dearth of great and original minds and turned in upon itself, and the stirring events of the world around it failed to ruffle its placid and indeed largely stagnant waters. It may be that if at La Flèche a vital Thomism had been taught instead of a desiccated scholasticism, Descartes might have reacted otherwise than he did and the subsequent history of western thought might have been different. In fact, the relationship between theology

and the new learning was for the most part one of ignorance or enmity, culminating in the open antagonism
between religion and science in the nineteenth century.
This meant that the immense advances made in such
sciences as medicine and psychology were likely to pass
the moralist by; man was coming to understand a great
deal more about his bodily and mental functions and
therefore his behaviour and its motivations, but the
moralist too often continued simply to scrutinize his
code-book, regarding the findings of science as an (often
disedifying) irrelevance.

Meanwhile what of the physicians and psychologists?
The subordination of practical science in general to religion, axiomatic in the Middle Ages, had by the time of
the Reformation to some extent ceased to be acknowledged in practice; thereafter the split widened and came
eventually to be justified in theory. Political theory developed in the direction of liberal individualism; economics, of *laissez-faire*; other sciences followed a similar
path: Descartes had split the psycho-physical unity of
man, Gassendi had gone back to the atomism of Democ-
ritus, Hobbes (who noted the 'frequency of insignificant
speech' at the scholastic Oxford of his day) had found an
answer to the problem of sensation in materialist terms,
Locke led on by easy stages through Berkeley to Hume,
metaphysics died, there was nothing left but materialist empiricism and the sciences became autonomous while
accepting in fact the postulates of the prevailing material-
ism. It was no longer thought, as Descartes had suggested,
that the soul resided in the pineal gland: there remained
simply the pineal gland. And with that the materialist
sciences were competent to deal in their own sphere. But
the next step was obvious: science could now on its own
assumptions claim to provide a complete explanation of
experience; religion was brushed aside as outmoded obscurantism, equated with barbarism: the heyday of omnicompetent science had set in.

From that mood we have to a great extent recovered. As Mr. Aldous Huxley put it : 'We are living now, not in the delicious intoxication induced by the early successes of science, but in a rather grisly morning-after, when it has become apparent that what triumphant science has done hitherto is to improve the means for achieving un-improved or actually deteriorated ends. In this condition of apprehensive sobriety we are able to see that the con-tents of literature, art, music—even in some measure of divinity and school metaphysics—are not sophistry and illusion, but simply those elements of experience which scientists chose to leave out of account, for the good reason that they had no intellectual methods for dealing with them'; and whereas formerly most scientists be-lieved 'that the product of their special incompetence was identical with reality as a whole' this belief has now begun to give way to 'a different and obviously truer conception of the relation between science and total ex-perience'.

But the struggle between religion and science contin-ues, if not so much now as a pitched battle between two opposing camps, at least as an inner disquietude in the consciences of individuals. Science (let us loosely say) will advocate contraception, sterilization, artificial insem-ination, euthanasia ; religion will disapprove of them ; the individual may find himself caught in a painful dilemma even though he has strong religious convictions : why is this so ? Partly at least it may be because, while at the conscious level we are fully aware of the limitations of science, unconsciously we cannot fully shake off the feel-ing that it 'must be right'. Science, we know, is con-cerned with facts and with the patterns-of-facts which we call physical laws : it can give us knowledge about these facts, it has no competence whatsoever to tell us how, or if, to use our knowledge. It can tell us how to do things ; it cannot possibly tell us whether or not we ought to do them. But the long reign of assumed omnicompetence lingers on, like its materialist postulates, in a sort of unconscious atmosphere which is difficult to dispel; and here therefore it is science which must be blamed, and blamed not merely for going beyond its sphere of competence but even for failing within its sphere of competence, for being unscientific—for it is unscientific for science to claim omnicompetence and therefore autonomy.

It seems then that, historically speaking, both moralists and scientists have been in their different ways to blame; but the fact remains that clashes do occur between the two spheres of thought and the important question is what we can do about them. Two answers suggest themselves.

First, it looks as though some clashes are both unavoidable and irremediable, not because of any fault either in scientists and moralists or in their respective disciplines, but simply because life in general and human nature in particular are *untidy*: we are fallen creatures living in a fallen world, and it is presumably to this fact that we must attribute certain undeniable and uncomfortable untidinesses in human life as we know it. For instance practical difficulties—not necessarily and certainly not exclusively moral ones—arise (to illustrate from the sphere of physiology) because it just is a fact that the graph of sexual development usually reaches its apex in men at one stage of life and in women at another; and that in adolescents the sexual urge develops physically long before their psychological development is sufficient to deal with it really adequately: in the same sort of way there are cases of physiological or psychological maladjustment —or for that matter quite simply of adverse circumstances —in which it is perfectly correct to say that what the sufferer *needs* physiologically or psychologically or just 'humanly speaking' is this or that or the other but that the principles of morality make it impossible: once again the untidiness, the irremediability, is not the fault of anyone or any science but is simply due to the fact that human nature is to a great extent disorganised, that the different

levels of the personality do not march together and sometimes, short of a miracle, cannot be made to.[2]

But that is not the whole story; and an at least arguable
second answer is that there is real need of clearer definition of the exact nature of each of the spheres of thought
and *therefore* of the relationship between them : for the
relationship between legalism and *scientisme* must obviously be quite different from that between let us say
Thomist ethics and a science which acknowledges the
existence of metaphysics and the fact of its own scientific
limitations.

Theology is no more omnicompetent than science; it
is not a self-sufficient closed system ; it concerns man's last
end and the way in which he is to reach it, and that way
includes events in the world of space-time and man's
attitude to them and judgement of them, an attitude and
a judgement determined not by some theological principle operating *in vacuo* but by a theology using the data
of the relevant sciences in order in the end to form a
prudential judgement about this particular action of this
particular individual in these particular circumstances.
Moral theology lays down general principles, and these
are essential to the living of the good life, but they cannot
be slapped straight onto an individual action like the cata-
plasm of Dr. Slop onto Susannah : the principles have to
be applied, and this is the work of prudence, and with
prudence as with art, as M. Maritain has pointed out,
each case is really a unique case which therefore in the
last resort can be adequately apprehended only in an
intuitive judgement.

Now the human person, like the human action, is an
individual unity; but in the concept of unity there are two
elements[3] : first, the one thing is by reason of its unity
distinct from other things ; secondly the one thing is by
reason of its unity one in its own internal structure, not
an agglomerate of diverse elements but a unity wrought

---

[2] cf. *infra*, chapter 7.   [3] cf. *infra*, chapter 11.

out of diverse elements. A man is not, as Descartes thought, an angel in a machine : matter and spirit are not two things in him but two elements constitutive of one thing. *Mens sana in corpore sano* must mean more than that a sound body is a useful instrument for the mind, for the body is not merely something which the mind uses or in which the mind resides ; you cannot influence one level of the personality without affecting other levels ; you cannot adequately study the psyche apart from the body or the body apart from the psyche. And since the striving for all immediate, secondary ends must clearly be governed by the striving for the ultimate end, which is theology's concern, it follows that to apply science in defiance of theology is to do violence not only to theology but to science itself, as a physical culture for example which produced bodily strength at the expense of mind and soul would be poor *physical* culture, bad for the *body*, because the perfection of the human body is essentially one element in the perfection of the human personality.

This leads to the question whether there can be such a thing as Christian medicine or psychology or for that matter physical culture ; and the answer is both yes and no. You cannot bring principles of faith or theology into scientific judgements without destroying science : when the doctor says, This is the best way to cure measles, the theologian as such is incompetent to argue the matter. But if faith and theology have nothing to do intrinsically with scientific judgements they can have a great deal to do with them extrinsically, for the thinker is not a disembodied mind but a man, the whole man. Faith can affect reason extrinsically by offering it a lead in matters where it would otherwise be baffled, as in the realm of mystery ; it can affect it also inasmuch as it orientates the whole man in one direction rather than another, so that while scientific judgements in themselves remain independent, the way in which they are viewed and applied may be fundamentally affected. Theology has no competence to interfere in scientific studies as such, but of its nature it must be concerned to regulate them extrinsically *ex alto* by subsuming them under the ultimate principles which govern man's pursuit of his destiny.

And the scientist, in submitting to such regulation, is not submitting to a set of externally imposed laws which bear no relation to those of his own science: he is submitting to a *Weltanschauung* in which his own laws play an organic part, for as soon as he begins to deal not with abstract but with applied science he is in touch with a reality larger than that of his own domain, and just as an economic which concerns itself with the false abstraction of 'economic man' is a faulty economic, so an applied physical science which concerns itself with the false abstraction of the purely animal man is a faulty science. But because his own laws are subsumed into a larger synthesis there emerges the principle on which any conflict must be decided, namely, that the lesser principle has meaning and validity only in the function of the higher, and where two or more lesser principles conflict it is by reference to the higher that the conflict must be resolved.

Often a conflict between morals and medicine will be found to have arisen either because medical principles have been isolated from their context in the totality of the philosophy of man, or because moral principles have been invoked without reference to the hierarchy of principles which gives them meaning or without due consideration of the individual character of the situation. Things will always go wrong, conflicts will always arise, if medical science insists on going beyond its own proper confines or if moral theology loses itself in unreal abstractions and codifications; and if one were asked to say in a word what tendencies, on the one side and the other, seem most likely to prevent a proper relationship between medicine and morals one would be tempted to say a sort of paternalism in the former and a spirit of legalism in the latter.

In an earlier age the mantle of the exiled priest was sometimes assumed by the poet, as when the puritan, anti-prelatical Milton abjured the delights of sporting in the shade with the Amaryllis of lyric poetry and became instead the *vates*, the prophet-priest, and turned what Johnson called the gigantic loftiness of his natural port to the service of a stern moral mission. Nowadays, it would seem, the mantle is more often to be found on the shoulders of doctor or psychiatrist. In February 1958, when the British Medical Association had been protesting vigorously against a series of television documentaries dealing with medical matters, a letter in *The Observer* voiced what seemed to be a not uncommon reaction : 'I suspect their protest is prompted by unconscious jealousy over the invasion by the public into the domain of the medical mystery and fears that their quasi-priestly authority—granted this has its therapeutic uses —may be lessened.'[4] There are two things which no doubt any specialist in any field must find difficult : one is to see the subject-matter of his studies in a wider framework than that of his own researches; the other, to avoid, when his own subject is mentioned among laymen, looking owl-like and making pontifical pronouncements. In the case of the doctor, as the above letter points out, there are times when an assumption of quasi-priestly authority may be therapeutically advisable; but sometimes the assumption is not so readily justifiable. A priest once went to a doctor for some medicine for an affection of the throat and, instead of medicine, was given a lengthy homily on the moral advantages, for character-training, of giving up smoking. Not unnaturally, and somewhat sharply, he told the doctor that he had come to him solely for medical help, the only kind that lay within his competence as a doctor : if he wanted moral advice he would go to someone qualified to give it. The full piquancy of the situation was however lost on the

[4] *The Observer*, 16th February 1958.

doctor, who did not know that his visitor was not only a priest but also a distinguished professor of moral theology.

One does in fact from time to time come across sufficiently disquieting evidences of a kind of medical paternalism, quite different from the giving of the wise counsel one associates with the 'family doctor': and such evidences are always a question of acting *ultra vires*, of acting not as medical practitioner but as psychologist or moralist or priest.

Some psychiatrists, it would seem, are yet readier to assume a god-like omniscience, not merely therapeutically for the benefit of their patients but in their own minds; and this can, to say the least, be very dangerous indeed. One has known of definite examples of this. A few slick questions, a homily, and the patient is dismissed, typed and taped—and sometimes the taping is so wide of the true mark as to be ludicrous if it were not tragic. Yet how much more delicately, and fearfully, those who practise this infant science should tread than the physician who at least has centuries of trial and error behind him! Professor Eliade has remarked that 'Freud thought of himself as the *Grand Eveillé* whereas in fact he was but the last of the positivists',[5] and this basic misconception seems to be reflected in the bland and facile assumption of something like omniscience and omnicompetence—as though it were a matter of what the theologians call infused knowledge, or indeed that mystical insight which enables the saints to penetrate in a flash the secrets of men's hearts—which is sometimes to be found among his followers. Pope Pius XII, in an address to the Thirteenth Congress of the International Association of Applied Psychology, while clearly stating that 'modern psychology, considered as a whole, merits approval from the moral and religious point of view', gave an equally clear warning to psychiatrists against going beyond their sphere of

[5] cf. *Images and Symbols*, p. 14.

competence, interfering with the rights of the individual, and in general failing to remember that psychiatry must be governed by moral principles : 'Morality teaches that scientific needs do not in themselves justify any and all ways of using psychological techniques and methods, even by serious psychologists and for useful ends.'[6]

But it must be admitted that the moralist too can sometimes be slick, superficial, too ready to pigeon-hole, admonish and dismiss. True, as priest his role is essentially different from that of doctor and psychotherapist : there are moments in which he is God's immediate representative, in the confessional for instance, and then he can —he must—hope that God will somehow speak through him and will not allow his appalling inadequacy, mental and moral, to damage and hurt those who come to him. There are times when he must speak 'as one having authority', and then the authority is not just that of an expert, if expert he be, but of one with a divine mandate. Yet how easy it is for him to overstep the bounds of his mandate, to fall a prey to an all too human love of power, to dictate when he should only guide, to forget that the task of a spiritual director is precisely to be directive, not preceptive, not to impose on souls the *onera importabilia*, the intolerable burdens, of the Pharisees but to help, encourage, console, inspire. And if in the immediate context of sacramental confession he must walk with fear and trembling, the same is true in degree when he is acting outside that immediate context, as preacher and teacher, moralist and adviser, or again when he is involved not in the immediate sacramental union between God and man but in the external juridical machinery of the Church. Most of us, alas, are far removed from the penetrating vision of a Curé d'Ars : we cannot read men's hearts ; but at least we can be at pains to remember always that they are there to be read, that it is hearts with which we have to deal, not entries in a ledger, and

[6] cf. *The Tablet*, 19th April 1958, p. 373.

that where hearts—unique, living personalities—are concerned the textbook tags of the legalist are not enough.

Thank God, for every officious doctor, every arrogant and slick psychiatrist, every priest to ride rough-shod over his penitents, there are a host of humble men, fully aware of their own limitations, their own lack of omniscience within their own sphere and in no doubt as to their lack of qualification to step beyond it. But it seems worthwhile to emphasize this need of humility, this determination not to assume a right to act *ultra vires*, because on this above all depends the possibility of a true *rapprochement* between medicine and morals.

And there is so much work to be done. We can indeed say, gratefully, that an immense amount has been and is being done; but an immense amount still remains; and so much depends on the ability to see a problem in a wider context than that of one's own specialist field while at the same time refusing to dogmatize outside that field. For a surgeon, for instance, the temptation to perform a craniotomy must sometimes be overwhelming if he thinks simply in terms of the immediate human situation, the saving of the happiness of man and wife and home; but he has to look to wider horizons, to realize that to do the operation means arrogating to himself the power of life and death, means in hard fact the taking of a human life, being a killer. For a moralist the temptation can be the opposite one : to cling to his textbook rules and ignore the human situation even though, as we have seen, a moral problem cannot in fact be adequately judged apart from its human situation. Indeed, of doctor, psychiatrist and moralist alike it can be said that they will inevitably fail in their duties unless in their different ways they always, all the time, respect and do justice to the human situations with which they are confronted.

There is a world of difference between paternalism and fatherliness. In varying degrees the latter must characterize the dealings of the doctor with the sick and suffering in body, the psychotherapist with the sick and suffer-

ing in mind, the priest with the sick and suffering in soul.
Once, after giving a broadcast talk, a priest received a
postcard, presumably inspired by the fact that he had
been introduced with the title 'Father', on which was
written in block capitals the simple message : 'Call no
man your father upon earth, one is your Father which is
in heaven. *Matt.* xxiii, 9.' It is interesting to speculate
about how the writer addressed and referred to his
earthly begetter. Fatherliness but not paternalism must,
in the Christian view, be present to some extent in every
exercise of authority : it is one of the things which prevent power from corrupting; but more than that, it is one
of the things which can bring together those who wield
authority of different kinds, as do priests and doctors,
provided always that fatherliness towards patient or penitent goes with a profound humility towards, and acceptance of, the authority of God, the eternal Father of
all.

When priest, physician and psychotherapist do thus
work together, each keeping to his own domain, with
understanding of and respect for the competence of the
others, and all holding the same fundamental religious
principles and having the same creative, humanist approach, then their work can indeed be fruitful. A man
will ask the priest for advice about his moral problems ;
the priest realizes that these problems are not simply
moral ones but are bound up with a psychological condition which needs expert help, and also that because of
this condition his visitor is also in poor physical condition, suffering from acute insomnia and so forth. He will
then call in his colleagues : the physician will cope with
the immediate physiological needs and disabilities; the
psychotherapist will set about the task, not merely of
'sweeping and garnishing' so as to leave an empty
house, but of helping the patient to adjust and integrate
his life within the framework of creative religion; the
priest, as moralist and confessor, will be guided by the
insight he gains from his colleagues and adjust his own

procedure accordingly. The patient for his part will have no need to fear either being preached at by the doctors on the one hand or, on the other, having his psychological problems dismissed by the priest with a curt exhortation to pull himself together and say his prayers. The three heads will be far more likely to succeed than would any one of them alone; but only if they thus cooperate, with understanding and respect for each other, for the patient, and above all with humble acceptance of the over-riding claims of God.

4. THE CONFESSOR'S PROBLEM

Psychiatrists are sometimes poor psychologists: they may have science but lack art; and so they may make some elementary blunder because, though they know all that the textbooks can teach them and can pin the appropriate type-labels on to their patients, they cannot see the personality and therefore the particular needs of this or that individual as such: they lack intuition. We have been thinking of the different functions of physician, psychotherapist and priest: obviously, between the last two in particular there are similarities as striking as the differences (though they must not be pressed too far) and this danger is one of them. For the confessor too needs art as well as science; when he has assimilated all that his books of moral theology and canon law can teach him his preparation is not at an end but only beginning. If he is to do his work properly he must learn how general principles are to be brought down to particular individual circumstances, how general rules must be adapted to the conditions and needs of X and Y. *Sacramenta sunt propter homines*: the sacraments were made for men: but the old axiom means precisely 'made for this man and that man', and every human being is unique. All this is especially applicable to the task of the confessor, is indeed the core of the confessor's problem; and it applies to every aspect of his work: as father, as doctor, as teacher, as judge.

The aspect of fatherhood is primary and must colour all the others. In the moment of absolution the priest, acting in the place and in the power of Christ, is the giver of life: he represents therefore the fatherhood of God the Creator and Re-creator of life; he must act then not merely with the authority of a father but with a father's understanding, patience, indulgence, love. In the Canon of the Mass we pray that God our Father may look upon our offerings *propitio ac sereno vultu*—as Msgr. Knox puts it, 'with an indulgent smile'; Pope Leo XII reminds us that the priest, having 'put on the mercy of Christ Jesus, must know how to deal carefully, patiently, and gently with sinners; for "charity is patient . . . , charity suffers all things, endures all things".' No doubt there are moments when it is proper for those who represent Christ to exhibit a just anger as he did; but the symbol of the sacrament of penance is not the driving out of the traffickers from the Temple but the episode of the woman taken in adultery. 'Go in peace': that is the end to which everything must lead; and so there can never be room for disgust, astonishment, reprobation, pharisaism: only the loving warmth and welcome of the father in the story of the prodigal—but with this in addition, that the priest must always realize that as a private individual he is a prodigal too.

This last point is capital. Just as we can never help anyone in any real sense if we minister *ex alto*, with the chilly condescension which kills all sympathy, so the priest can never help the sinner if the sinner is for him a stranger as remote from his own experience as an intruder from Mars. Consequently, for priests so graced by God that they have no immediate acquaintance with grave sin in their own lives the first duty is to use their imaginations, to see how easily they could stand where others stand, and to realize that if in fact they are different it is simply because he who is mighty has done great things in them; it is moreover to reflect on the ambiguity of the word 'sinner' and on how silly it is to think of the pharisee as sinless and the publican as sinner.

That is not to say that it can ever be right for the confessor to minimize the gravity of what is in itself grave; on the contrary it may at times be his duty to try to increase the penitent's sense of sin and sorrow for sin. Yet even so the end remains the same : to send him away in peace of soul : he must urge him and help him to sorrow, not remorse : to something creative, not sterile, to the sort of sorrow which is somehow simultaneously joy because the sense of sin is also at the same time a sense of God's love and mercy, and the darkness is that creative darkness in which the Light is found, adored, loved.

But this in its turn demands great understanding and gentleness. It will never be achieved if there is any element of repulsion or condescension; it will not be achieved merely by some understanding of human weakness in general. You cannot help John or Susan simply by having general scientific knowledge of boy or girl, man or woman, you can help only by having also some sort of intuitive understanding of this boy, this girl, this man, this woman. It is not for nothing that we speak of Holy *Mother* Church :[1] as our concept of God's fatherhood will be faulty if we exclude from it the qualities we associate in our human categories with the idea of motherhood, so we have to remember that, as Msgr. Bougeaud put it, just as there is something priestly about the heart of a mother, so there must be something of motherhood in the vocation of the priest, something of a mother's tenderness and compassion, but also something of her deep intuition where her children are concerned. A good mother is never shocked, never loses patience, never abandons her son, precisely because she understands him and understanding can sympathize—can console and encourage. ' Go in peace ' : the test of whether the confessor is really fulfilling this aspect of his office lies there : does the penitent go away restored, re-created, encouraged, no matter how deep his degradation or how hopeless his situation has seemed ? *Non veni vocare justos* : our Lord came to call sinners, not the just : but to call them to renewal, to hope, to the taking up of life again with fresh courage and strength and joy.

[1] cf. my *The Paradise Tree,* chapter IX.

There is something more which this aspect of fatherhood suggests. It is the vocation of parents, to help their
children to find and live their own vocations: to help
them, in other words, to grow up, to grow to maturity. In
the supernatural life as in the natural there are the stages
of infancy, childhood, adolescence, maturity; there are
the phenomena of arrested development, of life-refusal,
of childhood or adolescence never transcended. The
Church, not through her fault but through ours, *can* become a 'devouring mother': we *can*, if we are unwise
or cowardly, use her as an escape from life, we can hide
behind her skirts, we can try to throw back all our responsibilities upon her. If we do that we shall never live
our own vocations as Christians in the world; we shall
never bear witness to Christ; we shall never make use of
the talents given us; we shall never help to save the
world. The confessor, then, has two things to do. First he
must try as best he can to sense the 'age' of his penitent;
for he will have to act in one way towards the Catholic
of long standing and mature mind and soul, and in quite
another way towards the child in years, the recent convert, the timid soul incapable of making firm decisions
for himself and acting decisively upon them. Secondly,
he must decide whether for instance an infantile state
of soul is right and proper, is 'natural', in the circumstances, or whether in fact it represents a state of arrested
development, for again his treatment must differ accordingly: you do not treat a child in the way you treat a
mental invalid. In both cases maturity is the aim; but in
both cases also the aim remains peace; and so the confessor must avoid trying to dragoon an ailing penitent, to
make him go too fast; at all costs he must avoid treating a
real ailment of mind and soul as though it were a mere
fiction, something to be brushed aside with a single gesture. We know the irreparable harm that can be done by
the brash use of such slogans as 'Just pull yourself together'.

It is here that the second aspect of the confessor's office is most easily abused : that of judge. The confessional is indeed a tribunal : the penitent is the self-accused, the priest represents Christ the Judge, he administers the law and imposes sentence. But with what qualifications, what un-juridical colourings of the situation! For the judge remains first of all a father. To forget that is to drive people away from the sacraments : if the confessor uses his authority to browbeat his penitents, to harass them, to deny or belittle their difficulties; if he has an exaggerated idea of his own preceptive power; if he confuses objective wrongness with subjective guilt, and shows only impatience and incomprehension for the penitent's subjective situation; if he makes impossible demands; if he can express only blame, censure, disgust and horror; then he is failing in his ministry : he is not leading men back to God but driving them away from him.

It would seem to be a reflection on some of the representatives of the *ecclesia docens* that the *ecclesia discens* should so often accuse itself in confession of sins which are not sins at all—the Sunday Mass unavoidably missed, the harmless and indeed commendable love-making, the temptations never given in to—and attribute far more importance to a breach of ecclesiastical law such as Friday abstinence than to breaches of divine law, the sins against justice and charity. Furthermore there is the undeniable fact that so many Catholics think the really most important sins are the sins of the flesh. And one cannot help wondering to what extent a misguided technique in the confessional is responsible, when indeed it is not simply a question of a false scale of values in the mind of the confessor himself.

For instance, interrogation is sometimes part of the duty of the confessor as judge : but how carefully it must be done! The difficulty often is that for the integrity of the confession a question must be asked about some sin which is not at all the most *important* thing mentioned by the penitent : surely then it is wise in such cases to offset the question by some animad version about the more important matter, as a question for instance about the precise species of a sexual sin might be off-set by some remarks about the importance of being faithful to the duty of daily prayer. And how essential it is to be prudent in any questionings about sexual sins : *melius in pluribus deficere quam in uno superabundare*, it is better to ask too little in many cases than to ask too much in one; for here again, and in the whole matter of questioning in general, the confessor has to try to estimate the spiritual age of the penitent and to act accordingly. Indiscretion, where the young in age or in the spiritual life are concerned, can easily do great harm : can shock the penitent, can put ideas into his head, can confuse him, can set up a real and perhaps insuperable inhibition which will prevent him from going to confession again. (Here if anywhere the winds of the theological textbooks need tempering by the virtues of prudence and gentleness and by a fatherly insight.)

The penitent's age is again relevant when it is the penitent himself who asks questions. 'Was it a mortal sin, Father?'—how is the confessor to answer? He must of course, where objective right and wrong are concerned, answer quite simply : Actions of the type x are or are not mortal sins; but what of subjective degrees of guilt? Surely once again he must study the age of his penitent : the spiritually adult he must help to make up their own minds—You know the conditions which must be fulfilled if a sin is to be mortal—full knowledge, awareness, consent—were they in fact fulfilled in this case or not? At the other extreme there are the scrupulous, who by definition are incapable of making up their own minds : here is a case where the priest, if he is to be truly a father-judge, must shoulder all responsibility, must be categorical; his main concern here is therapeutic, to lead the penitent away from his ceaseless self-analysis, unreal and neurotic and sterile, to the love and mercy of God not as an abstract truth intellectually apprehended but as a lived experience. If he is wise he will restrict his penitent's confession to some simple, general formula from which there must be no departure: I accuse myself of all the sins I have committed since my last confession and all the sins of my past life; and for the rest he will go on reminding him again and again: God is your Father, not a policeman; think about God and his love, not about yourself . . .

But it is not only the scrupulous who have to be helped to guard against anxiety. A sense of sin and of guilt can be a creative thing, creatively used: can be the darkness, the dark waters—the parallel with baptism is obvious—out of which life comes. But if sin is allowed to breed anxiety the anxiety itself will breed further sin and the further sin may in the end produce despair, so that what is in fact just a moral difficulty like any other may become a crisis, a reason for turning away hopelessly from the sacraments and from the Church altogether.[2] Anxiety is one thing; tension is quite another. Tension is the condition of life and of growth: the fact that a penitent has this moral disability, this failing which he cannot seem to conquer, is no cause for despair; on the contrary, it is there to be used, to engage his energies, to provide the exercise without which he might become flabby and the 'divine discontent' without which he might grow proud and complacent.

Here the judge becomes the doctor: the priest's office is now to diagnose, perhaps to warn, certainly to advise. He must try to discern the cause of the trouble in order to suggest a remedy. To suggest: the advice of a spiritual director is meant to be precisely directive, not preceptive.[3] There is a danger here, on the penitent's part, of a sort of spiritual masochism: a surrendering of one's personality, one's mind and will, into the hands of another human being so as to escape from maturity and in the last resort from life itself; it is for the confessor, on the

[2] cf. *infra*, chapter 9.   [3] cf. *supra*, chapter 3.

contrary, to try to lead the penitent towards an ever greater degree of maturity: towards a more and more adult attitude to religion, in prayer, in worship, in the moral life.[4] Religion can so easily become magic, superstition, a seeking for comfort, for irresponsible security, an escape; and the human mind can be a very tortuous instrument. If we try, by the adroit way we put things, to manœuvre the priest into saying that *x* is not a sin (though deep down we know that it is) so that then, regarding his dictum as oracular, we feel we can sin with impunity; if we look to him to answer every question, to be a sort of continual source of private revelation, instead of using the mind that God gave us; if we look to him for a slick and immediate solution of all our moral difficulties: we are using him not as a minister of God but as a magician, we are misusing the sacrament.

It remains true that the confessor as doctor has often to try to suggest remedial measures; and again he meets the same difficulty as before: he is dealing with an individual. There are of course certain remedial measures for all moral difficulties: the sacraments, prayer, devotion to our Lady, to one's guardian angel, and so forth; there are particular types of remedy against particular vices; but what in the last resort is needed is *this* particular remedy for *this* man's particular failing. It is, alas, a fact that sometimes advice is given which falls into none of these three categories: to take an extreme case, a homosexual described in a letter to the author how he had been told in confession to 'find a nice Irish girl and marry her' and how, when he remained silent, the priest asked him if he disliked the Irish.

As doctor the priest must advise; as teacher he must instruct; but again with the same reservations. In order

---

[4] Examples of immaturity and the need of instruction readily suggest themselves from the sphere of sexual ethics, but are of course far from being confined to it; they are equally to be found in the spheres of social justice or prudence or fortitude.

to instruct adequately he must have a grasp of the science of moral theology; he must also have the art of discerning the needs and abilities and limitations of individual souls. Obviously he will fail in his duty if he withholds information which is necessary and which the penitent can assimilate; but equally he will fail if his instruction causes anxiety, scrupulosity, or bad faith. *Conscientiae non sunt inquietandae*—the conscience should not be disturbed needlessly; there are certain traditional guiding principles which help us to see how and when information may be given without danger of disturbing peace of mind and conscience.

Ignorance is either vincible (culpable and curable) or not. If the former, information about this or that obligation must be given since the ignorance denotes bad faith; but what if it is, as the theologians say, invincible? Here the confessor has to distinguish: if he feels convinced that the penitent will be able to understand his instruction and to follow it, he must give it; otherwise he must not (for it would be useless and he would simply be turning good faith into bad faith and material sin into formal sin) unless the penitent himself asks, or unless silence would be considered as an encouragement to evil, or if the ignorance or doubt concerns the first principles of the natural law or their immediate consequences (for such ignorance could not long be invincible and therefore excusable), or finally if lack of instruction would leave the penitent in proximate occasion of sinning. But *conscientiae non inquietandae*: in doubt, we are told, it is better to abstain; and the doubt, it must once again be emphasized, means primarily a doubt about the subjective dispositions and capacities of this or that particular penitent.

Conscientiae non inquietandae is the negative aspect of the positive purpose of the sacrament contained in the phrase, Go in peace. If instruction is not given it is in order that the penitent may quite literally be left in peace; if it is given it must be given in such a way as to stress its positive and creative content. Not just, This is something you must not do; but, This is to be avoided in order that that may be achieved. Nothing is more discouraging than a tirade about the importance of a negation. Battling against vices and failings has to be set in the perspective of an attempt to achieve the good life; and virtue itself has to be set within the supreme aim, which is charity or holiness. It is a good thing to be a man of high moral character, but not if it means a lack of love. Better to love God out of weakness than to love oneself in one's strength. Great charity is compatible with many weaknesses; but the most perfect moral probity does not of itself imply humility and love. Hence the problem for the confessor here is one of great delicacy: should he give instruction on this or that point or not? if so, in what way is it to be done? how can he put the emphasis on the positive without minimizing the negative? how can he stress adequately the importance of avoiding sin while at the same time giving a positive emphasis to all that he says? Finally, how can he urge the importance of moral effort while at the same time making it clear to the penitent that the one essential thing is not action but 'passion', that *pati divina* which is the root of holiness?

These are questions to which there is no slick answer; but they do not, as they stand, represent the confessor's problem in its entirety: they have to be put into the context of the over-riding problem with which we have already been concerned—the problem of adapting *all* decisions, judgements, advice, exhortation to *this* particular individual. And this might well seem to make the difficulties insoluble. For how can the confessor adapt himself to the individual penitent unless he knows the penitent; and how can he know him if he is no more than a transient whisper through a grille?

It should perhaps be made clear that in this chapter we have been concerned to keep within the terms of reference set by its title: no doubt in the great majority of cases there will be no particular 'confessor's problem':

the confessions of ordinary, simple, uninhibited people usually call for nothing more complicated than the giving of penance and absolution with perhaps a little homily if time allows. But we are concerned here not with the usual confessions but with the unusual; we are concerned with a problem because we are concerned with the Church's problem-children—and if they are a minority they are certainly not a small minority. Even the best-informed and most balanced of mortals need advice sometimes, need the ministrations of the confessor as teacher or doctor; and then inevitably the problem makes itself felt. Compare the priest, faced with an invisible, anonymous penitent and conscious of the long queue waiting outside, with the psychiatrist who learns gradually, through a long series of lengthy interviews, something about the individual with whom he is called to deal. How *can* the priest hope to succeed?

No doubt the ultimate answer is that he must rely on and hope for the requisite supernatural help in the form of some infusion of discernment and wisdom : that, after all, apart from the main work of absolution, is his share in the sacrament. But it would be wrong to rely upon grace alone : he is bound to take such natural measures as are open to him to make his task more feasible : what are they?

The first is to acquire a real understanding of the task itself. The priest who tells himself that he is quite adequately equipped because he knows all the textbook answers, all the moral and canonical tags, is headed for disaster. As we have seen, his job is also to make sure that he understands human frailty and sinfulness, not from some remote eminence, but from being acquainted with it, really or imaginatively, himself. He will never advise aright, still less encourage and strengthen, unless first he can sympathize; and he will never sympathize unless first he understands. *Nil humani alienum* has its application here more forcibly perhaps than anywhere else.

Secondly, he must think himself gradually into the

totality of his office : he may never be just the judge or the teacher; he must always be father and doctor as well. If he judges, it must be as a doctor looking to the health of his patient; if he instructs, it must be as a father striving to lead his son to maturity and to the achieving of his own vocation in the world.

Thirdly, he must learn gradually by experience. It might be supposed that a mere whisper must be entirely unrevealing of a personality : it is not so. Words are always revealing, whether whispered or not. A turn of phrase, an emphasis, an intonation, the whole way in which what has to be said is in fact said : all these can reveal the speaker : can reveal sorrow or cynicism or levity, self-complacence or humility, real trouble and anxiety or the lust for self-display, simplicity of heart or a hard-boiled over-sophistication, timidity or courage, maturity or infantilism . . . All these can reveal the speaker : but in very varying degrees. Sometimes it will be no more than a hint that is given, a probability suggested; and then with what care, what caution, the confessor has to proceed! That is why his two guiding principles must always be to say too little rather than too much, and to be above all things gentle. For if he says too much, or in saying even a little is brutal, he will do much harm; if he says too little but says it with true gentleness the chances are that his penitent will return, to increase his understanding of him and to give him an opportunity of offering further enlightenment, encouragement and help. At the very least he will have achieved the purpose of the sacrament : he will have allowed the penitent to go in peace.

To go in peace : two facts, sad but certain, have to be admitted and allowed for in all this discussion of the confessor's problem. First, there is the great and perhaps growing lack of peace in so many individuals in the world of today. Mention was made above of the simple, uncomplicated souls about whom there is no problem; but nowadays fewer and fewer penitents are likely to be wholly simple and uncomplicated, at least in countries such as ours. We live in an age of anxiety and fear; and these tensions once experienced are not likely to be confined to political or economic matters. True, religion *can* be the stabilising factor which minimizes and perhaps dissipates altogether the natural fears which today oppress humanity; but the thing can also work the other way round, and a person suffering from a natural sense of insecurity may easily feel its repercussions in the sphere of religion. Again, the conditions of life as we know it are likely to produce moral tensions and difficulties : one has only to think for example of the appallingly high incidence of moral problems connected with marriage—real problems to which there is just no easy solution, and sometimes no solution at all apart from heroic virtue.[5] Finally, we live in a climate of opinion the tendency of which is to make faith difficult and religion unreal. It may be assumed then that many penitents if not most will lack peace, quite apart from the sense in which any sin-laden soul may be said to lack peace until it has received absolution. Hence the phrase, Go in peace, assumes today a special significance, and its fulfilment is attended by special difficulties. To restore a soul to grace does not necessarily mean, nowadays, to restore its peace : it may well have to be led gradually to the point at which grace will in fact mean peace because it will in fact overcome the fears and anxieties, natural and supernatural, to which modern life has given rise.

But the second fact shows that this goal is far from being achieved : the fact that many Catholics—and again it is perhaps a growing number—leave the confessional with discouragement, depression, perhaps with resentment and rancour, in their hearts because of what they regard as a total lack of comprehension on the part of their priests. It just will not do—it is not enough—to tell the penitent that he must say his prayers and go to the sacra-

[5] cf. *infra*, chapter 7.

ments and all will be well, when he knows already from bitter experience that all will not be well. It just will not do to upbraid people for sins the avoidance of which would be tantamount to heroic virtue. And so we come back to one of the essential elements in the equipment of the confessor, one of the things without which he can never hope even to begin to solve his problem : the need of a sympathy based on a real and deep understanding of his penitent's difficulties. Without that the already terrifying gulf which separates clergy and laity must simply go on widening : on the one hand a laity battling with real and often heart-breaking problems and often looking desperately for guidance and help ; on the other, a clergy too often living in a quite different world, a closed world of their own, talking a language no longer understood of the people, and quite unable to reconcile the academic formulas they have learnt from their textbooks with the real problems with which those formulas ought, if they are to have any value at all, to help them to deal. It will be recalled that Pope Pius XII called upon theological students precisely not to be satisfied with absorbing the contents of 'little manuals' but to do some real thinking : and his words might well form the text for all courses of pastoral theology.

Da mihi intellectum: give me understanding: that must surely be the prayer of the confessor. Give me understanding of principles as opposed to rules of thumb; give me understanding of the difficulties which beset people in the world of today; and finally : give me understanding of the individuals, for otherwise I shall not be able to help them, and when they ask me for guidance I shall not give them peace, I shall send them empty away.

5. WHAT IS 'NATURAL'?

Few confusions are more common or more perplexing than that between two quite different uses of the word 'natural'; yet both uses are valid enough if rightly understood, and the distinction between them is a simple one.

On the one hand, we are always saying or hearing it said that this or that action, though not commendable, is 'natural enough' or 'only natural'. It is only natural for people to lose their tempers or their heads sometimes, only natural if occasionally they oversleep or overeat, only natural if sometimes they let this or that passion get the better of them. What does the phrase mean? It means, in effect, 'only to be expected'. And why is it to be expected? Because that, to use another common phrase, is 'only human nature' *as we know it*. But what is the human nature that we know in everyday experience? It is, in the language of Catholic theology, *fallen* human nature.

Fallen human nature means human nature not as it was created by God, not as it was intended to be by God, but as it exists now, warped and twisted by evil. It is not wholly evil, far from it; but the evil tendencies are there, as we all know from our own experience; in our better moments we realize that we ought to be conquering them, integrating the energies which find an outlet in evil actions into the organic unity of the good life; but again and again we fail, or we forget altogether even to try, and then nature-as-we-know-it has its way.

On the other hand, we hear a great deal about the requirements of what is called the natural law; and these requirements are always running counter to what in fact we regard as natural in the first sense. Why? Because the nature we are here concerned with is not the fallen nature of man, but the nature of man *in itself*.

Before attempting to elaborate this, let us clear away another source of confusion. The word 'law' too is ambiguous. In Britain the law bids us to drive to the left : it could perfectly well be changed tomorrow. In Britain the law enacts that bars must be closed except at certain restricted hours : it could perfectly well be changed tomorrow—and no doubt if we were more enlightened and civilized than we are it would be. These are cases of what is called positive law : an authority *lays down* the law, creates it. No human authority, however, can lay down or create the laws of physics : all that man can do is try to discover them. For these laws are not decisions made by man : they are statements of the way things in fact work, the way things *are*. Now the natural law is of this latter kind. It does not tell us about things which are right because they are commanded or wrong because they are forbidden : it tells us about things which are commanded or forbidden because in themselves they are right or wrong. And why are they right or wrong in themselves? Because that is the way things are : that is the pattern, not indeed of human nature as we know it, but of human nature in itself.

We return then to this idea of nature in itself. Let us start with an artefact for here there is no ambiguity of terms. What is the nature of a razor? We have our answer if we can concoct a *definition* : let us say, roughly, a razor is a steel instrument with a finely sharpened edge, capable of shaving the hair from the skin. At once it becomes obvious that, if that is its nature, it would be unnatural to use a razor in order to try to hack through an iron bar. In the same way it would be unnatural to keep (or try to keep) a cat in a pond or a fish in a cage. What then of man? A definition has come down to us through the ages : man is a rational animal. That is not an altogether satisfactory definition of man-as-we-know-him, because man-as-we-know-him is often an extremely irrational animal; but it does give us the essentials about the nature of man in itself: man is a psychophysical being, an animal capable of rational thought; and as a razor fulfils its definition perfectly when it is a good razor and gives a perfect shave, so man fulfils his definition, his nature, perfectly when he is a good-minded animal—a sound and healthy body expressing and obeying a wise and balanced mind.

Now a razor which had been used to hack an iron bar would be not unlike human nature-as-we-know-it. What the natural law states for us is simply that if we use our human nature in this or that way we shall end up like the jagged razor; if we use it in these other ways we shall end up by resembling the perfect razor inasmuch as we shall have at our disposal an instrument capable of achieving the perfect fulfilment of our purpose, our destiny as rational animals.[1] (This is obvious if we think for instance of the coarsening and finally the disintegration which sooner or later await the habitual glutton or drunkard or sensualist of one sort or another. On the other hand there are the equally obvious and equally disastrous effects of trying to treat human nature, as the 'angelists' do, as though it were not animal at all.)

Most people seem ready to agree that such things as wanton cruelty (an 'unnatural mother') or the degrading of human beings by torture or drugs or a sort of diabolical travesty of psychiatry are unnatural: the confusion between the two uses of the term does not worry them there, though in fact these things are alas to be expected of fallen nature. Where the confusion seems to cause the greatest muddle is in the realm of sexual ethics, especially in an age which bases its arguments or its prejudices so largely on statistical evidence. (What we need is less statistics and more hard logical thinking.)

[1] This cannot in fact be achieved without redemption and the grace of God.

'Everybody does it,' people say, fresh from their reading of this or that Report, 'so it *must* be natural.'

This is to make confusion worse confounded. All that the statistician can do is tell us what is or is not common or usual : the moment he begins to tell us what is or is not *natural* he goes beyond his chosen terms of reference. The usual is a purely statistical concept : it is simply what the great majority of people do or are. It is usual to have five fingers on the hand, to have eyes of the same colour, and so on. But it is dangerous, to say the least, to try to argue from the usual to the natural. In most times and places through the world's history it has been usual for men to be heterosexual; but there have in fact been times and places in which it was usual for them to be homosexual. It is best then to leave statistics, to leave the usual, out of account in this context and to concentrate on what is or is not natural.

In what sense is it 'natural' for men and women to indulge in extra-marital sexual adventures? In the sense already defined, it is only to be expected of our fallen nature. But in exactly the same way dishonesty, coward-ice, lying, cruelty are equally to be expected of our fallen nature, yet no one argues that because these things are thus 'natural' they are therefore permissible or good. What is the reason? Presumably because we have got so thoroughly into the quite un-Christian habit of mind which identifies immorality with sexual sin that we feel a need to justify or excuse our sexual vagaries but not our other immoralities. (Dishonesty? the question is whether we can get away with it. Cowardice? there are the con-ventions of course; one must not run away from the battlefield, but if I shirk a private duty because I'm a moral coward it's nobody's affair but mine.) In what sense then is promiscuity unnatural? Because human love is of its nature such that it can never reach its perfection ex-cept as the result of a long, gradual process of discovery and of fusion : a process in which sex has its essential part to play, but sex as an element in the total dedication, fidelity, loyalty, steadfastness, of the two personalities to each other.

To act in accordance with human nature means to respect human nature; but that in its turn means to respect all the various elements which go to make up human nature in its psychophysical unity. It is this which throws light on what is perhaps the most common example, in this sort of context, of the confusion we have been considering: the question of the use of contraceptives by married people. No one with any sense or sensibility will deny that for hosts of people today, unable for one cogent reason or another to have more children, the following of the law in this respect implies a burden, a hardship, of appalling severity. Why then is it the law? It is not the Church's law, in the sense of being a law of the Church's devizing: the Church states, and abides by, the natural law. Why then is it the natural law?

Here we return to the razor. When we say 'respect for human nature' we mean respect for all the elements which make up human nature. Therefore we mean respect for the functions and organs of human sex. But human sex, because it is human, exists so to speak on more than one level: it is biological, as in all animals; it is personal, an instrument in the making of love, as it is not in all animals. Therefore we must respect both levels. We cannot, without being unnatural, use it as a purely animal function, a purely bodily pleasure in which the heart is in no way involved. On the other hand we cannot, without being unnatural, treat it purely as love-making without respect for its biological level: if we do, we are going 'against the nature' of the thing, the function, just as in maltreating the razor we are going against the nature of the razor.

There is in this context the old, stale gibe about the safe-period, that the Church forbids contrivances but permits contrivance. It may be a clever debating-point; but it shows a complete failure to grasp the principles of the matter. We do not maltreat the razor by not using it at all but only by using it in a way which destroys its purpose. We do not maltreat the biological function of sex by not using it (i.e. by intercourse at a time when the biological function is probably infertile) but by using it in a way which destroys the purpose of that function. And that this latter is indeed unnatural in the strict sense is made clearer by such collateral arguments as the fact that so many people find it in practice to be aesthetically repugnant, and repugnant also in a deeply personal sense—an interference with the freedom and spontaneity and generosity of love.

The same confusion is to be found in the question of homosexuality. People talk about 'unnatural vices'; but the homosexual will argue—and again quite rightly if the terms are rightly understood—that what would be 'unnatural' for him would be heterosexual intercourse. Homosexual intercourse of one sort or another is indeed, for such a man, according to his nature-as-he-knows it : why then should it be wrong? Because, once again, it is not according to the nature of sex as such : it destroys the biological purpose.

But, people will argue finally, there is plenty of evidence of homosexual practices among animals : and you must surely admit that the animal world is natural in your sense : animals at any rate do not sin against the natural law. No, animals do not sin ; but they are not left unscathed by sin. Nature 'red in tooth and claw' is warped and twisted too ; so St. Paul speaks of the whole of creation groaning and in travail ; we cannot expect a world in which the mystery of iniquity exercises such power to remain itself immune from the influences of that power.

It is a great pity that Christians talk so much about 'moral laws' when in fact they mean these statements of the facts of human nature as such, for it too often means in practice that they think of these laws as arbitrary dispositions which sometimes at least, in hard cases, can and ought to be modified or dispensed with. There are cases where the fact that two and two make four and not five is extremely hard; but you cannot for all that change the nature of things. The same is true with these moral principles—the great fundamental principles from which all moral theorizing and all practical judgements have in the last resort to proceed. The Church cannot unsay the ten commandments; what is so desperately needed today is an understanding and sympathy on the part of those who represent the Church towards the often intolerable burdens which unnatural circumstances, economic and otherwise, place on the shoulders of those who are trying their best to keep the commandments and who therefore, if they fail, need encouragement rather than censure, and who, if they succeed, must often be regarded as having achieved heroic sanctity.

6. DESIGNS FOR LOVING

'What is this thing called love?' The question has been debated times without number: by the great poets, philosophers, mystics; by alert little logicians and portentous statisticians; by playwrights, novelists, songsters; and of course by lovers of various kinds, from those who indulge in a fever of passionate introspection to the simpler souls who sometimes briefly wonder in a bemused and befogged sort of way what has hit them. The plain man may find himself confused by the variety of often conflicting answers given to the question, the variety of names given to the experience or to different aspects of it. In his *Moral Values in the Ancient World* Professor John Ferguson discusses such concepts as the Greek *eros, philia, philanthropia, homonoia*; the Latin *amicitia, pietas, humanitas*; and the Hebrew *chesed* and '*ahabah*—the former of the last two being the steadfast, covenanted loving-kindness of God and *pietas* of man, the latter the deeper, unconditioned love that has in it something alike of *eros* and of *philanthropia*; and he shows how the two worlds of thought, the Jewish and the Graeco-Roman, were fundamentally different and could impinge but little on one another until Christianity brought to the world its new inspiration, its new concept of love, and what was in effect a new word to describe it: *agape*.

A great deal of discussion has centred on the difference, and the relationship, between *eros* and *agape*; but again the discussion has led to confusion because of the varying interpretations or emphases put on the words by various writers. Some have seen the two simply in terms of a contrast between getting and giving, between a love that is selfish, possessive and greedy and one that is selfless and undemanding. But this is altogether too *simpliste* if one admits that the 'divine frenzy' of Eros can inspire to deeds of heroic self-sacrifice or on the other hand that there is a sense in which it is true to say that 'there is a yearning in God that needs satisfaction',[1] that Eckhart was right when he said that 'God needs man' and Julian of Norwich right in speaking of the 'love-longing' of Christ.

Others have put more stress on the idea of *eros* as an irresistible 'fate', a tyranny, a madness; the literature of the world, ancient, medieval and modern, is indeed full of this theme, but it is clearly a mistake so to restrict this to the concept of *eros* as to make *agape* by comparison seem a coldly reasonable affair. The erotic imagery of the *Song of Songs* is traditionally applied to mystical love; and it is to the same sort of imagery that the mystics themselves turn to describe their experiences. Nor can one hope to define holiness—as opposed to rectitude—in terms of what is coldly reasonable and right. And if, as Professor Ferguson remarks,[2] when St. Ignatius cried 'My Eros is crucified' he was referring to his own sensual nature, and it was Origen who interpreted the word as referring to Christ, still the identification was accepted, and became part of the traditional language of mysticism.

A similar antithesis appears in the discussion of love and marriage. It will be remembered that M. Denis de Rougemont in his *Passion and Society* approached the problem of 'romantic love' historically, from the study of 'courtly love', of Catharism and Manicheism, and from the examination of the Tristram-Iseult theme and its derivatives. For him, the antithesis as it exists for us today is clear-cut indeed: 'Passion and marriage are essentially irreconcilable. Their origins and their ends make them mutually exclusive. Their co-existence in our midst constantly raises insoluble problems, and the strife thereby engendered constitutes a persistent danger for every one

[1] Ferguson, *op. cit.*, p. 224. [2] *ibid.*, p. 101.

of our social safeguards.'[3] Mr. William P. Wylie in his
The Pattern of Love borrows from Professor C. S.
Lewis the term 'Mother Kirk' to describe 'all those institutional
christian bodies and individual persons who adhere to
the traditional doctrine of marriage as handed down by
the Western Church', and notes her 'curiously equivocal'
attitude to 'the sexual side of marriage': on the one
hand the glorification of marriage as a sacrament, on the
other hand the puritan streak in so much Christian thinking, the legalist emphasis (the 'insistence on the *legal*
side of marriage as apparently the only thing that matters, the only thing the Church will worry about'), and
again the 'widespread idea that sexual sin is the worst, if
not indeed the only, sin, and the even more widespread
idea that all forms of extra-marital intercourse are equally
sinful'.[4] It may—indeed must—be said that these last two
ideas are no part of the Church's teaching; it remains
true that they are in fact widely accepted as such, and it is
difficult to explain this apart from a misplaced emphasis
on the part of some representatives of the official teaching and, in the matter of the equality of extra-marital sins,
on an exclusive preoccupation with the legal, as opposed
to the human, aspects of behaviour—for in fact it is obvious enough that there is a world of (moral) difference
between a loveless, commercialized sexual act and a
truly loving, though illicit, union of lovers.

Mr. Wylie devotes much attention to the idea of 'recognition' in explaining the phenomenon we call 'falling
in love'; the lover seeing in the person loved, as Charles
Williams puts it, 'the life he was meant to possess instead
of his own', or, in Professor Guitton's phrase, the person
loved seeming 'to be familiar even before being known'.[5]
But here again confusion appears, the doctors disagree:
'that there is such a thing as "love at first sight" few

<hr>

[3] Rougemont, *op. cit.*, revised edition 1956, p. 277.
[4] Wylie, *op. cit.*, pp. 2, 14, 21.
[5] *Essay on Human Love*, pp. 80–1.

would be prepared to deny', writes Mr. Wylie; for Rougemont on the other hand love at first sight and the 'irresistible' nature of passion are merely 'tropes of a romantic rhetoric';[6] once again everything depends on just what one means by 'love'. Mr. Wylie can appeal to the *stupor* which fell upon Dante, as it had doubtless fallen upon innumerable human beings, in the moment of meeting and 'recognition'; but Rougemont can rightly claim that 'if desire travels swiftly and anywhere, love is slow and difficult':[7] what we have to ask is whether, when we speak of falling in love, of being in love, and of loving, we are using the word each time in the same sense.

One can in fact hold that love at first sight does happen without being thereby committed to regarding the love as irresistible fate; Fr. D'Arcy's criticism of Rougemont was precisely that he left no room for any intermediate (Apolline) love between the dark pagan Eros and supernatural *agape*, nor explained how *eros* can be transformed into *agape*;[8] Mr. Wylie on the other hand surely overstates his case when he writes of the Church trying 'desperately hard' to keep religious experience and romantic love apart,[9] but he does clearly state that the transformation of the latter into *caritas* is precisely the end at which human love should aim.[10]

The fact is that if we are dealing with the calmer forms of affection, with *philia* or *philanthropia* or *humanitas*, we feel we are on solid ground; we can at least to some extent see clearly; once we get into deeper waters we tend to feel lost in hopeless confusion; for humanity *is* in confusion; at any deep level human reality and experience are wildly untidy, and the untidiest thing of all love which, whether as the *eros* of sexual passion or the *agape* of the mystics' union with God, refuses to be fitted into

[6] Rougemont, *op. cit.*, p. 134.   [7] *ibid.*, p. 313.
[8] *The Mind and Heart of Love*, p. 40.   [9] Wylie, *op. cit.*, p. 115.
[10] *ibid.*, p. 133.

neat formulae or abstract theorizings. The historical thesis that 'romantic love' somehow appeared for the first time in eleventh-century Provence can only be accepted, if at all, after we have ruthlessly purged the term of many elements normally associated with it. It certainly cannot be equated with *eros*; *eros* and *agape* themselves seem to refuse to keep in an orderly fashion to their respective sides of the fence; nor can we equate them, as a contrasting pair, with Dionysus and Apollo, or with darkness and light or death and life or desire and *benevolentia*.

If we set all theorizings aside and start simply from the data of our untidy experience we seem constrained to say that a love which can truly be so called—that is, which is not a mere matter of chemical reactions, of lust, of fantasy, of narcissist-projection—does come to human beings in a variety of ways and guises, in varying degrees of suddenness, of force, of depth, of irresistibility, of calmness or frenzy, of idealism or earthiness, of hunger and selflessness, and may be found to have as its object almost anything from the immensities of the Godhead to a bedraggled rag-doll or the dents and wrinkles in an old boot. We seem constrained moreover to go on to say that like most if not all sublunary realities—and even our sublunary apprehensions of divine reality—it is a paradox, and therefore cannot be understood unless we fully accept and grasp the two sides of the paradox. Professor Ferguson may argue that *eros* in its inmost nature is 'the love that gets not the love that gives';[11] the fact remains that in authentic love as we know it the distinction is blurred if not abolished; there is both getting and giving and the giving is a form of getting, the getting a form of giving. The same is true of the distinction between selfish and selfless, once the fact is learnt and lived that the highest self-realization is to be found in the selflessness of love; or between possessed and possessing, since where

[11] Ferguson, *op. cit.*, p.101.

there is real love there is an equality underlying all differences and each of the lovers is both possessed and possessor. The same love may include—and perhaps in its perfection fuse—the frenzy of *eros*, the reasonableness of *philia*. Even that death-wish which has been seen as the logical outcome of the frustrated desire of *eros* for complete fusion can find some sort of echo in the longings of *agape*—did not St. Paul long to 'be dissolved' and be with Christ?—for the infinity of desire is as true (though in different senses) of the one love as of the other.

From the kind of love that is so overwhelming as to be comparable to possession by a *daimon* to the placid, uncomplicated affection of simple souls at the other extreme there is in fact an infinite variety of kinds and degrees of love; and in the Christian view of things there seems to be no reason why any of them should not be transformed into *caritas*, provided only that the people concerned are prepared to accept the realities of the situation however paradoxical and perhaps unpalatable. Professor Ferguson, criticizing the pagan ideal of autarchy or self-sufficiency, notes how in *Peer Gynt* the motto of the trolls is 'To thyself be enough' but of the humans 'To thyself be true', and adds that 'however flounderingly the humans might behave, we cannot but see it as the nobler and higher aim'.[12] The tragedy is that we flounder intellectually as well as morally; without knowing it we deceive ourselves, we lose sight of reality, of the truth, and so come all too easily to living in a fantasy world while allowing real living and loving to pass us by.

It is for this reason that books such as Dom Aelred Watkin's *The Enemies of Love* are so helpful. Dom Aelred does not of course deal only with these 'enemies'; but the discussion of them lies at the heart of his book; and the point of immediate concern to us here is that they are enemies of love because they are enemies of truth, of the

[12] Ferguson, *op. cit.*, p. 158.

truth or reality of love itself. The harrowing sense of insecurity—Does he or she really love me?—makes us demanding of proof and so makes us forget the truth that depends upon giving 'not indeed without hope of return, but without consideration of return'—for love is not 'something that just "happens", it is something that has to be made', and that is the way of its making. The same sort of thing is true of jealousy, of possessiveness, of self-indulgence (as turning the loved person into a means, not an end, and so destroying the reality of love); most obviously of all it is true of 'false romance', which leads us not to love a real human being (or for that matter a real thing) but to create an 'entirely imaginative and fictitious picture' and to worship that, or to create a similarly unreal picture of what love should be like and to blame the other person involved when we find the fiction inescapably confronted by the reality. 'Love should not be blind . . . We have to learn that it is through things as they are that God works and love grows.'[13]

But if the total reality is accepted, loved and lived, then indeed *eros* can be transformed, can be integrated into *agape*, though it will not be done quickly or easily. Whatever we may think of the possibility of an instantaneous 'recognition' we must surely agree with Dom Aelred that 'love's complete happiness' cannot be achieved without labour and tears.[14] We shall be on the road to the fullness of reality only if we can accept what seems to be the pattern of all created reality as we know it: the birth of life out of death, of light out of darkness. This, certainly, is the pattern of the soul's progress in the love of God as the mystics (elaborating and applying our Lord's words about the grain of wheat and the mystery of rebirth through the dark waters) describe it for us; and a line in a responsory in the breviary puts the process very succinctly (and at the same time describes the course of

---

[13] Watkin, *op. cit.*, pp. 69, 72.   [14] *ibid.*, p. 72.

many human love-relationships) when it speaks of the
soul first catching sight of God (*quem vidi*) and falling
in love with what it glimpses (*amavi*), then trusting
(*credidi*) when darkness succeeds the flash of enlightenment, and then finally loving with the deeper love which
is called *dilectio* and which has in it the element of deliberate choice—'my beloved, chosen out of thousands'
—and therefore the steadfastness, the covenanted commitment, of the Jewish *chesed*, the love that as Professor
Ferguson points out finds its tenderest expression in the
story of Osee, the love that 'is not broken when the one
loved turns aside'.[15]

From *amor* to *dilectio*, from *eros* to *agape*: the more
perfect love is born, in darkness, out of the less: it trans-
forms it; it does not abolish, it integrates. As Christians
we are meant, not to make a picture of God's love by
cutting it to the pattern of our chaotic experience of
human love, but to decide what human love ought to be
like by comparing it with what we can discover of the
uncreated Love. And of that we discover something from
the Bible in general and the picture of the incarnate Word
in particular, and from the lives and the love of the saints.
Both sources show that what we think of as the *eros*-qual-
ities of love have certainly not disappeared: we find here
something dangerous and fierce like the pentecostal wind
and fire, unpredictable like the wind that bloweth where
it listeth, prodigal like the woman with her pot of precious
spikenard or like the father of 'the prodigal' in the
parable; we find a love at once tender and terrible; unconventional, as Christ was unconventional; not 'respectable', any more than Christ was 'respectable' when
he consorted with publicans and sinners; a love that is
disorderly, if order is to be defined in terms either of
worldly prudence or of a smug decorum. Professor Ferguson rightly contrasts sanctity with the 'philosophy of
safety' (though his interpretation of the Aristotelean doc-

15 Ferguson, *op. cit.*, p. 219.

trine of the golden mean may be questioned[16]); the Horatian *est modus in rebus* is no motto for a saint; holiness is not merely superlative justice or righteousness; the Christian moral life is based on the virtues but it includes also the gifts and fruits of the Spirit, the supra-rational 'divine instinct' or impulse, the mighty Wind and Fire whose effect was to make the onlookers think that the apostles were drunk—and the well-known prayer, *Anima Christi*, contains the phrase *inebria me* which in fact means 'make me drunk'.

Yet, however high his mystical soarings, the Christian can never leave the pedestrian path of virtue, of the ten commandments; his behaviour may be supra-rational, never irrational; the 'frenzy' must be divine, not sub-human; and the greatest heights and depths of *caritas* are always characterized by those 'calm' qualities of which St. Paul speaks in his panegyric: *caritas* is always patient, kind, trustful, enduring, never envious or insolent or proud . . . The paradox is maintained: our Lord in the Gospel constantly speaks of rewards, yet St. Catherine of Siena is rebuked for her egoism when she expresses her longing for heaven; God's love for us is prodigal in its generosity—'while we were yet sinners, Christ died for us': the love, as Professor Ferguson points out, 'is not conditioned by human merit'[17]—yet he is none the less a 'jealous God', a 'burning and consuming fire'. Even in regard to the basic issue of the goal of love, of fusion or union, there is paradox rather than an opposition of con-

[16] It is quite true that 'you cannot have too much goodness' (p. 40); but that is surely not what the doctrine implies. You can fail in courage either by defect (cowardice) or excess (rashness); but the excess is not (using words strictly) an excess *of courage*; it means that the energies which might have been the *material* of an act of courage become, because for example of excessive precipitation, the material of an act of foolhardiness; once one has so to speak found the formula of true courage then of course one cannot have too much of it.

[17] Ferguson, *op. cit.*, p. 219.

traries: St. Paul's 'I live, now not I', St. Catherine of Genoa's 'My Me is God', the story of St. Catherine of Siena's change of hearts with Christ, the very phrase 'living in love' or the word of John Donne, 'interinanimation', the mystics' description of the soul as *scintilla Dei*, the spark coming out of and having to return to the eternal Fire, or again what Professor Guitton has to say of the discovery of the greater self through learning to live in the divine 'erosphere'[18]: all these seem to imply something deeper, more radical, perhaps more catastrophic, than the word 'union' (as opposed to 'fusion') need suggest; and, as we have seen, the way to this goal is darkness, is a kind of death—Christ's themes of the grain of wheat, of the losing and finding of life, the self-naughting of the mystics; the traditional Christian word 'mortification' which has a so much wider content than the Greek *askesis*—so that to desire the goal involves desiring the death-darkness that leads to it, implies then a sort of death-wish.

But this death-wish *is* a life-wish: the aspect of fusion (or of duality or union *with*), for if a love-relationship ceased to be a dialogue, a *communicatio*, and became instead a devouring-and-being-devoured it would cease to be love. The fusion-aspect in isolation is indeed death because unreality, fantasy: in integral love a real (though not physical, not 'ontological') death and real death-wish are there: but it is a 'death', a darkness, accepted as the means to that life which is to be the final word.

If then with Kierkegaard we say that as God creates *ex nihilo*, out of nothingness, so he reduces us to nothingness in order to make something of us even now; if with Thomas Merton, echoing a host of mystics and spiritual writers, we say that a man must be poor and stripped and naked before the water and the Spirit can re-create him; if, stressing the 'erotic' element in the Christian process, we remember that 'Eros is passion' and that the

---

[18] Guillot, *op. cit.*, pp. 82–3.

very word suggests that a man in the power of Eros 'is an object not a subject, a sufferer, not an agent' if we recall the Greek vase which depicts Eros moving 'with powerful wings over the face of the waters' like the brooding Dove of *Genesis*—for Eros 'is the great urge by which the year renews its life' and in some of the very oldest religious mysteries 'the cult of Eros was fused with that of the Earth Mother'[19]—if we recall all this we must also recall that it is only one aspect of the paradox: there is the calmer side, the lighter side (using the word without levity), the Apolline side, patient, reasonable, gentle, the side of unassuming commonsense and above all of humility—for humility is truth, accepting the facts about ourselves, accepting (among other things) the fact that in the sphere of *caritas* we are not cut out to be eagles like John the Divine any more than in the human sphere we are cut out to be among the world's Great Lovers . . . Not eagles but sparrows; and God does not demand of sparrows the epic soarings of eagles. But if we may recall this side for our comfort we must also recall it as a warning against the danger of any turning of the acceptance of darkness into a cult of darkness—or for that matter the danger of thinking that all is lost unless we *feel* the divine fire burning within us, *feel* possessed by a divine frenzy.

The Christian can never accept *surtout point de zèle*—any more than he can accept compromise or the cult of safety—as his ideal; he will only distort and diminish love, whether of God or of man, if he tries to rid it of its 'erotic' elements. On the other hand he will miss the whole point if he thinks of it as exclusively or primarily a matter of feeling.

'To be in love is not necessarily to love' says M. de Rougemont,[20] and at first sight the statement may look puzzling, we may feel it would be truer to turn it round the other way. But he continues: 'To be in love is a state;

[19] cf. Ferguson, *op. cit.*, pp. 76–80.
[20] Rougemont, *op. cit.*, p. 310.

to love, an act. A state is suffered or undergone : but a
act has to be decided upon'; the commandment to love
the Lord our God 'can only be concerned with acts. It
would be absurd to demand of a man a state of *sentiment*.'[21] This 'being in love' then is not the same thing
as Dante's *essere in caritate*. Again, Mr. Wylie says that
'from being *in* love' lovers 'have to becoming *loving*';[22]
and he means that from belonging merely to each other
they have to grow into belonging to God and therefore
to love : they must 'in a sense become love itself': and
again it is this latter which is *essere in caritate*. Professor
Ferguson is closer to Dante (because to St. Thomas)
when, also distinguishing between state and acts, he says
that love is 'in its first sense a state, an attitude, a spirit,
an alignment of the personality, what Aristotle would
call a *hexis*',[23] that is, a *habitus* or virtue—for virtue is
not essentially a question of what you feel but of what
you will and do.

Yet once again we have to beware of one-sidedness.
To say that we are not commanded to *feel* loving is not
to say that feelings are unimportant, still less that we can
make a purely unemotional rectitude our ideal. Dom
Aelred is here again very much to the point : 'Rectitude
unaccompanied by affection is seldom inspiring, sympathy without real human feeling is seldom convincing':[24] and if it is doubtful whether most of us would get
far in forming a virtuous habit unless we had sometimes
the appropriate feelings to help us, it is certain that we
cannot exclude the emotional life from the concept of
living in *caritate*, for *caritas* must affect in some degree
every level of the personality, must in the end remould
the personality as a whole. It would be a tragic mistake
to confuse *benevolentia* with the somewhat impersonal,
chilly, perhaps even condescending implications of the
word 'benevolence'; Italian lovers say *ti voglio bene*,

---

[21] *ibid.*, p. 311 (italics mine).   [22] Wylie, *op. cit.*, pp. 117–18.
[23] Ferguson, *op. cit.*, p. 231.   [24] Watkin, *op. cit.*, p. 85.

and it means literally 'I wish you well' but it also means infinitely more than that.

Let us return to the subject of marriage and—not Mother Kirk now but—the Church, Christianity. What ought we to do as Christians in face of the present breakdown of marriage in our society? What is our best defence of Christian marriage as an ideal? Certainly the worst thing we can do is to encourage the idea that for us marriage is a purely juridical or legitimate or legalistic affair, or that the Church is timorous or grudging in its attitude to passion : we have to expose the hollowness, the sham, the emptiness of 'false romance' by putting something positive in its place, by showing forth the reality and depth and richness of Christian passion, of *eros* and *agape* made one; we have to show forth *eros*, not as a 'mighty god', but as an aspect of the mighty God, and the mighty God crucified. How can we do this in view of the Church's 'intransigent' emphasis on the legal, the contractual? If holiness and conventionality are incompatible, how can the ideal of a holy and happy marriage and conventionality be compatible? The answer is that at all costs we must avoid confusing convention with covenant, with troth, with choice or *dilectio*. M. de Rougemont may or may not be correct in saying that 'when marriage was established on social conventions, and hence, from the individual standpoint, on chance, it had at least as much likelihood of success as marriage based on "love" alone'; he is surely right in holding that in the last resort (since in the last resort, when all ponderables have been duly weighed, the shape of the future—even of the future I and the future Thou—is unforeseeable) 'everything depends on a *decision*':[25] but a decision, a choice, an act of *dilectio*, a covenant, *not* a convention. Nothing could be more unconventional than the marriage of Osee, but his love triumphed because like God's love for Israel it was a 'love of commitment',

[25] Rougemont, *op. cit.*, pp. 294, 304.

a covenanted love. Perhaps it is true that, if ecstatic happiness is made the criterion, most marriages are either
total or partial failures, the best of them achieving only
a sort of jog-trot equanimity; if the covenant is kept
through the darkness of disappointment or tragedy it may
be that the greater fulfilment will come in the end : the
patience of the covenanted love may produce a more
perfect work than an endlessly unruffled happiness would
have done.

Covenant and love (but not conventionality and love)
are thus like law and freedom in St. Paul : Christ came not
to abolish but to fulfil the law by turning it from a bondage into a liberation, and it becomes that when it becomes part of oneself, internalized, integrated, by love—
of the law or the Lawgiver or both. Law or covenant without love means bondage; love without law or covenant
means chaos and catastrophe; law-as-love or love-covenanted mean both freedom and permanence because
steadfast choice, *dilectio*. And love-covenanted includes
passion-covenanted; so that (if we interpret 'morals' as
meaning 'purely conventional moral standards') we can
adopt M. de Rougemont's definition of marriage as 'the
institution in which passion is " contained ", not by morals,
but by love'.[26] For continence is of little moral value unless it is positive in purpose; and this is part of its purpose : the channelling, deepening, personalizing of passion in husband and wife, so that it is allowed to become
neither a selfish, isolated pleasure-seeking on the part of
the one or the other, nor a preoccupation with each other
to the point of excluding other claims upon them. Another part of its purpose is of course to restrict the expression of passion (in deed or in heart) to the terms of the
covenant; but this too is essentially positive since it
means on the one hand the continued creation of all that
is involved in the covenant and on the other hand the
ability to accept and sanctify—and therefore be enriched

[26] *ibid.*, p. 315.

by—other affections instead of allowing them to become destructive infidelities.

Professor Ferguson translated *teleioi* in our Lord's injunction, Be ye perfect, as 'all-embracing', noting that while this does not exhaust the meaning of the word it is included within it.[27] *Essere in caritate*: to come to the love of all: that is the goal of Christian *caritas*; and into that quest any authentic love, if its unruly elements are 'contained', can be integrated. We start from the fact that all that is, is of itself holy, coming as it does from the hands of God: all sin therefore, as Dom Aelred puts it, 'must partake in some measure of the nature of sacrilege',[28] just as all sin should be seen less as a transgression than as a rebellion against God, against Love.[29] And it is the sin, the rebellion, that is privation, life-refusal, non-being. There would doubtless be less of a chasm between the Church and the world if we were more at pains to proclaim, and live, the positive content of our heritage, the humanness of our ideal of holiness. 'Charity cannot exist in a vacuum apart from any expression of it in human experience, while purity is a positive quality of love and not the mere negation of lust. The love of man, provided it is love, cannot conflict with the love of God, for love cannot war against itself.'[30] And it is the paradoxical totality of love that has to be affirmed and lived if we are to fulfil the Christian pattern and to become 'all-embracing' and complete: it is *eros* and *agape* together, *eros* integrated into *agape*; there are both darkness and light, death and life, pain and joy, frustration and fulfilment, as long as we remain *in via*, pilgrims on our way; but what we have to believe and proclaim is that this mingling of light and shadow is not final, and that if we are loyal to our covenanted loves divine and human we shall come in the end to gaze on, and for ever live and rejoice in, the 'everlasting splendour'.

---

[27] Ferguson, *op. cit.*, p. 235.   [28] Watkin, *op. cit.*, p. 12.
[29] Ferguson, *op. cit.*, p. 214.   [30] Watkin, *op. cit.*, p. 88.

7. ANOMALIES AND GRACE

Nowadays the grim fact has to be faced that problems connected with the sexual life, often caused by a clash between the individual Catholic's instinct or indeed conviction on the one hand and the Church's teaching as it is so often presented or understood on the other, are responsible not only for great unhappiness in the lives of innumerable Catholics, but also for the fact that an appalling number are led, by their inability to 'conform', to leave the Church altogether. It seems equally to be a fact that within the Church a growing conviction among lay people that the clergy sometimes fail to do justice to their very real difficulties is leading to a cleavage between the two.

The problem of birth-control, as we have seen, is an obvious example. There are married people who for one reason or another just cannot, at least temporarily, have more children : it is not helpful to tell them, *sans façons*, that in that case they must just 'abstain from indulgence in sexual intercourse'. (Ecclesiastical jargon often indicates a lack of real theological thinking.[1]) The point is that this is not a question of 'indulgence' : it is of the essence of their married, their Catholic married, life. From the layman's point of view what too often happens is that first they are told how wonderfully God has blessed the mystery of human love and sex and marriage, and then in the next breath they are told to go off and do without it. The first thing they must be made to see is that the Church does not regard abstinence as a 'solution' for them : that in fact, apart from the restriction of

[1] cf. *infra*, chapter 12.

intercourse to the 'safe period'—and this, for one reason or another, is not always possible or desirable in all cases —there is no solution. We are living in a very unnatural sort of world; and in consequence what is natural for us, and therefore good, is sometimes impossible.[2] If in these unnatural circumstances they can manage, when all else fails, to achieve abstinence together in union with the sufferings and the sacrifice of our Lord, they are achieving heroic virtue, which means something like sanctity, and they should be told so. But to demand this heroic virtue of them with the easy nonchalance or the impatient curtness with which one might command a boy to stop stealing apples from an orchard is to do a grave disservice to God and man alike.

But it is not only in marriage that painful and often insoluble difficulties arise. Every human being has his own individual psycho-sexual make-up and therefore his own individual difficulties. Quite apart from the normal problems of adolescence there are the various adult problems which beset the heterosexual, the homosexual, the bisexual, the 'intersexual', the auto-erotic; there are all the more or less pathological manifestations of the sexual instinct; and each of these needs understanding and sympathy if guidance is to be given, and it must be positive and creative guidance if anything of value is to be achieved.

What could be more discouraging to anyone of whatever age or 'type' who is struggling with his or her particular difficulties, than to be blandly told by someone who presumably has no experience of any such difficulties : *gratia Dei sufficit*—go to the sacraments, and the 'grace of God is sufficient'? The plain fact as they see it is that the grace of God is not sufficient, for they go to the sacraments, they go on trying, yet their difficulties continue. This does not mean that we must not quote

[2] cf. *supra*, chapter 5.

St. Paul to them : it does mean that we must explain him. In the same way we must not water down the Church's teaching about sin : we must explain it; and above all we must explain that the struggle against this or that tendency is a part of something much greater and wider, the struggle for something, and that this in its turn is essentially a struggle not to do something but to be something—to be taken into, and possessed by, that torrent of life and of love which is the Christ-life on earth.

Grace is indeed sufficient : but for what? Not to do away with all difficulties instantly, or after a short—or perhaps a very long—period, for it is not magic. It is sufficient, given good will, courage, perseverance, to transform the personality gradually, slowly, but surely till it becomes ensouled by love. The difficulties may even then continue, materially speaking, but they will have lost their sting, their malice : they will not kill or quench the life that has been received.

But if they continue at all in any sense must it not mean that victory has not been achieved and that therefore grace has not been sufficient after all? No, the whole point of this life is that it is struggle not victory, not *quies*. Our idea of what this struggle is has been largely falsified : we tend to think of the Christian life as a struggle against immorality and immorality as a question of sins of the flesh, and where these latter are concerned the issue seems clear-cut : as long as I continue to commit these sins I am enslaved; once I have stopped committing them I am victorious. (Even so it is not quite so simple as that : one might for instance have achieved continence but not chastity, which incidentally could sometimes be a very dangerous state of affairs.) But let us take the case of charity, the most important of all : if we could say we no longer committed any sins against charity, should we then have achieved victory? In a sense, yes indeed, beyond the dreams of most mortals; but still only in a sense. Charity consists not in an abstention but in a state of being—of being in love with God and his creation; and love can go on growing indefinitely, so that here we should not have achieved victory until we had achieved the fullest measure of love of which God had made us capable.

That the struggle continues therefore is no cause for despair or even despondency : it is the condition of life. Nevertheless, the Catholic will cry, you tell us that x is a mortal sin and that if I commit it and die I shall go to hell : so how does all that help me ? It helps because it will rectify just that way of looking at things, which is a falsification not only of the nature of morality but, far worse, of the nature of God. If x is a mortal sin it is always a mortal sin objectively speaking : but the more you struggle against it the less likely it is in each successive case to be mortal subjectively speaking; and the more love of God there is in you the less likelihood there is of any sin at all being mortal subjectively speaking— because the less there will be in you of deliberate malice and the more of mere frailty. And quite apart from all that, do you really think that God, who is love and who died to save us, could do as you imply : could ignore a man's struggle however unsuccessful and wait till he had fallen and then pounce upon him ? You must not of course begin to minimize sin on that account or to adopt a false optimism : on the contrary it is essential to try to deepen and deepen your sense of sin in general, its true nature, its horror, the way it hurts God. But at the same time you must try equally to deepen your sense of God's mercy and love and understanding, and your humble hope in them.

A well-known book and film have made us familiar with the motto, 'Never take no for an answer'. An analogous motto might well find its place on the title page of every book of pastoral theology : 'Never give don't for an answer'. Nothing so fills people with discouragement and perhaps in the end despair as to have to listen to violent diatribes about the heinousness of this or that mode of behaviour without one word of constructive advice or encouragement. There may be, there often is, no real solution to a human problem : there is always something constructive and creative to be said about it.

It is a heartening thing that the outstanding work of the *Cahiers Laënnec*, in which doctors, psychiatrists and theologians collaborate in a truly constructive approach to these problems, is now available in English.[3] Here, on the medical side, is a treatment of such problems as adolescent masturbation, homosexuality, artificial insemination, as humane and constructive as it is scientific ; and, on the part of the theologian-contributors, a truly theological approach, matter-of-fact, sensitive, always creative—the larger issues, the ultimate ends, never lost sight of in concern for the immediate moral judgement.

What help can be given to those weighed down by such problems as we are here considering? (There are of course people who are quite happy about their own particular sexual tendencies and have no moral scruples about finding the requisite outlet for them : we are not concerned here with them but with those for whom these things are indeed a problem and who need help and ask for it, sometimes desperately.)

In the case of adolescent masturbation one might have thought that at least the evil days of scaremongering tactics, of the threat of insanity and so forth, were over ; but the editor of these translations makes it clear that at any rate in some places this is not so. Even if it were, however, there would still remain the type of 'treatment' which consists in alternatively thundering about the moral evil and degradation involved, and feeding to the young (to quote the editor again) that sort of 'pious literature which extols the virtue of holy chastity in poetic and floral terms'—a literature which as he rightly says

[3] *New Problems in Medical Ethics*, ed. in English by Dom Peter Flood, o.s.b. Tr. from the French *Cahiers Laënnec* by Calachy Gerard Carroll. Mercier Press.

'does not appeal to modern youth and offers therefore no help in their difficulties'.[4]

It may be just as important to make it clear that masturbation is 'natural' for a boy, in the popular sense of the word,[5] as it is to explain that it is not natural in the philosophical sense of the word. It is 'natural' for him because he has become conscious of new potentialities in himself and wants to experiment with them and, having experimented, to continue enjoying the satisfaction they afford, at a moment in his evolution when he is not yet capable, even though he is well informed theoretically, of seeing and feeling these things as part of the much bigger and greater mystery of human love, for he is still in his auto-erotic stage of development. Later, if as so often happens, he passes into a homosexual phase it will similarly be 'natural' for him to want to share his satisfactions with his friends. We have to make it clear then at the very beginning that he is not a freak or a pariah (if he is in any danger of thinking so) and that we realize that what he is doing is (again in the popular sense of the word) 'natural enough': without this, anything else we can say will fall on deaf ears: the old insupportable tension between the Church's (apparently) arbitrary *fiat* and what seems reasonable will be set up in his mind.[6]

But having made this clear we can go on to show how sex, not because of some ecclesiastical or religious *fiat* but in the nature of things and by common consent of all humanity, is to be regarded as perfect in itself only when it is an element in something much greater: that total and unrestricted mutual self-giving which we call love. 'It is admitted by the majority of sexologists that full personal realization is found, when there is a sexual relation, only in components fully respected . . . It is for

---

[4] Flood, *op. cit.*, vol. i, pp. 4–5.   [5] cf. *supra*, chapter 5.
[6] This is further discussed *infra* chapter 9: *The Problem of Pseudo-Vice.*

us to show (the adolescent), with Hensard, that "sexual pleasure is indeed simply an increase of being . . . a source of true joy only when it has ceased to be partial and aberrant, when it has been raised to a love capable of altruism and tenderness".[7] Thus he may be brought to see that auto-eroticism is not natural in the true sense of the word precisely because it is the isolation of one element from its human totality and is therefore, even from the point of view of sexual pleasure itself, partial, imperfect.

But even if all this is acknowledged the difficulties may continue; and then the essential thing is to underline the fact that this is but one difficulty to be dealt with bit by bit, among a host of others—laziness, lying, dishonesty, greediness—and that growth in the Christian life as a whole does not depend on an instant or even a quick solution of this particular problem. Young people some-times seem to cease practising their religion simply be-cause they cannot 'conform' in this matter: but as we have seen, if they ended this struggle there would still be many others, for struggle is the condition of life—and would they leave the Church simply because they could not control their tempers, their curiosity, their greeds of one kind or another? If we thus put this particular prob-lem into a more general setting, a more reasonable light, then, but only then, we may hope to break the vicious circle[8] by getting rid of the anxiety bred by the sense of guilt. 'To exaggerate the importance of commonplace masturbation at the time of puberty is to compromise its disappearance and to show the subject that there is here a manifestation of a sudden development of his sexuality which must be transitory if he wishes to become, as he aspires to do, a man in the full sense of the word.'[9]

All this is very far from saying that the moral signifi-

---

[7] cf. Flood, *op. cit.*, vol. I, pp. 8, 18.
[8] Failures produce anxiety: the anxiety itself produces other fail-ures.   [9] Flood, *op. cit.*, vol. I, pp. 14–15.

cance of masturbation is to be brushed aside as unimportant: on the contrary, its importance will be underlined the more the importance, the value, the mystery, of sexual life in its fullness is stressed. But if the priest for his part realizes, distinguishing as always between objective and subjective, how small the measure of responsibility, of deliberation and malice, may be, he will set himself at all costs not to 'overwhelm' the sinner. Indeed, he would thus only increase the sentiment of inferiority of which masturbation is often merely the symbol. On the contrary the psyche must be consolidated and strengthened, the heart must be opened, respect for self developed and confidence in the possibility of self-conquest re-established.[10]

The same sort of approach is still more necessary where there is question of sexual aberrations such as homosexuality[11] which cause profound distress and produce problems which seem insoluble. As Père Charles Larère remarks: 'The first condition of effective spiritual cure rests in the *greeting*. It is very difficult for the invert[12] when he faces up to admitting his inversion. The priest must therefore be very understanding, but discreet and considerate, in his first questions, awakening confidence before going on to speak of spiritual remedies. With many patients, the fact of being able to speak of it openly for the first time without seeing the pharisaic look or the look of naive astonishment on the face of his listener is already the beginning of a cure.'[13]

---

[10] Flood, *op. cit.*, vol. I, p. 41.

[11] The word 'homosexuality' is so often inaccurately used nowadays that definition is advisable. It means simply a psycho-sexual orientation towards one's own sex; more simply, a tendency to fall in love with people of one's own sex rather than or instead of the other; it does not of itself imply any form of sexual activity. To use the word to mean sexual acts between individuals of the same sex is slipshod and misleading; to use it (as is sometimes done) as a euphemism for anal intercourse between heterosexuals is absurd.

[12] i.e. the homosexual.   [13] Flood, *op. cit.*, vol. I, p. 116.

The root cause of many tragically unsuccessful encounters of this kind would seem to be that the one from whom help is sought has never been taught the absolutely essential distinction between psycho-sexual deviations on the one hand and the sexual sins to which they may or may not give rise on the other. There is nothing at all disgraceful, still less morally reprehensible, about homosexuality: the homosexual can justly point to the long list of great men of his stamp—philosophers, statesmen, warriors, painters, poets—who have done so much to benefit humanity. But in the second place, even where there is sin, though objectively speaking when it is homosexual it is graver because more unnatural than when it is heterosexual, still from the pastoral point of view there should be just as much sympathy for the homosexual who from weakness falls into his particular sin as for the heterosexual who falls into his.

We are not concerned with the various different forms of homosexuality ('there is no such thing as homosexuality as such') nor with its etiology. From the pastoral point of view, the important distinction will be between the homosexual who wants to be cured of his inversion and the one who does not and cannot. In the first case, if the homosexual has in fact been giving way to his sexual impulses, the priest will co-operate with the psychiatrist by doing his best, as Père Larère points out, to break down in the subject the 'idea of the fatalism of his vice, an idea which usually obsesses him', and by encouraging him not to waste his energies brooding over the extent to which he is responsible for his falls—'If the question is a legitimate one . . . any answer which tends to finality is useless'—but gradually to 'cultivate and strengthen the grip of conscience'.[14]

[14] *idem*, vol. I, p. 117. In cases where the penitent is suffering from a real obsession, e.g. some form of sexual fetichism of obsessional force, it may be useful to help him to make a clear distinction in his own mind between acts which are thus plainly determined—in which case he should try not to brood over them afterwards but on

What of the second case? It may well prove necessary at the beginning to try to cure the homosexual of self-pity. It is unjust, he will often argue, that through no fault of his he should be debarred as a Catholic from all sexual life. It must be pointed out that many heterosexuals are in like case—men, for instance, who cannot marry the woman they love—and perhaps in worse case, for at least no moral principle debars the homosexual (as circumstances may debar the heterosexual) from the companionship of the one he loves, or indeed from such outward manifestations of affection as are neither sinful in themselves nor productive of sin.

That balance once established it remains, as with the problems previously considered, to give him confidence and a sense of creative achievement. He may need much encouragement if repeated failures are in question and, as so often happens, he is tormented by his sense of guilt and failure. The story of the woman taken in adultery can be put to him in terms of his own life, and the seventy times seven, and the whole idea of struggle as outlined above. He is the victim of a bad habit, but every ordinary Catholic is the victim of some bad habit or another—and in the last resort which is worse, his own failing, in which there may at least be a great measure of love and self-giving, or, for instance, the black-hearted spite and hatred and denigration of others which is sometimes to be met with among the *bien-pensants*?

He must be encouraged to receive the sacraments as often as possible; to give some time every day to mental prayer, and especially to try to live in God's presence—to 'practise the presence of God' as the usual phrase has it

---

the contrary at once turn his mind resolutely to other things—and other similar acts which however are freely chosen : it is these that he must seek to eliminate. And it may well be wisest for him to direct his sense of guilt, not on to these acts, of either kind, so much as on to his sinfulness in general, his lack of love and faith and zeal. But for this whole question of obsessive behaviour, cf. *infra*, chapter 9.

—and in general to concentrate on the positive task of trying to love God more deeply, to understand more deeply God's mercy and to share as far as he can in the daily redemptive work of Christ in the world. He must be made to see his love not as something condemned but on the contrary as something which can be of great value to him in helping others of his own sex, giving him as it does an insight and understanding and patience in his dealings with them which he would otherwise lack. He may need help in finding some creative outlet, without which he must necessarily be frustrated and unhappy, for if he can be brought to see that, 'according to the fine formula of Maranon, who cannot be accused of pursuing a metaphysical aim, "true sexual activity is neither sexual deviation nor the union of the sexes but creative work in the case of the man and maternity in the case of the woman",'[15] he may be able not merely to find peace and happiness himself but to do much to bring peace and happiness to others.

He will do much more than that if he can be helped to pour his whole life, deliberately day by day, into the great descending flood of Christ's redemptive pity for mankind. 'I emphasize,' writes Père Larère, 'the sufferings of these souls, often endowed with great wealth of feeling and real spiritual understanding . . . And if there are few among them who can long sustain such tension of their whole being and accept the constant effort towards spiritualization to dominate this divorce between mind and body, it sometimes happens that souls are met with who have gained magnificent spiritual profit from such a struggle. Indeed, when once they have recognized the gravity of this deviation and accepted the painful struggle that has no ending, it happens that this anomaly becomes, for these men, the occasion of a very exalted spiritual life.'[16]

[15] Flood, op. cit., vol. I, p. 18.
[16] Flood, op. cit., vol. I, p. 120. cf. p. 207.

8. THE PROBLEM OF PSEUDO-VIRTUE

One of the fundamental problems confronting the moralist today is that of the concept of unconscious motivation and its integration into the theological analysis of human action and of the discussion of the ideas of responsibility, guilt and merit. Such discussion cannot nowadays take the idea of *finis*, 'end', simply and solely as comprising ends which emerge into consciousness: it must also take into account ends of which the agent is unconscious or which at least are not wholly clear to consciousness.

At first sight one might feel reluctant to accept this statement as valid; for we rightly think of a *finis in intentione*, a willed purpose or objective, as existing only in our knowledge of it. But we must surely accept the findings of modern depth psychology at least to the extent of admitting the reality of a kind of knowledge which does not rise fully to the level of consciousness. We may be disposed to look upon Freudian theory (and, for that matter, the practice of some at least of his followers) with an unfriendly and sceptical eye, but it would be ridiculous obscurantism to deny the reality of his empirical findings; similarly it would be absurd to belittle the importance to the moralist of the Jungian 'map of the psyche'. It is no longer reasonable to question the fact that a great part of our psychic life lies below the level of consciousness; and psychic life must be taken to include cognitive as well as affective activities: perceptions, apprehensions, memories as well as impulses, inclinations, feelings.

There is admittedly so much that is ill-defined and uncertain in our knowledge of the unconscious that we are in no position to dogmatize about its nature and the manner and conditions of its functionings; but at least we can say that what seems to distinguish conscious from unconscious psychic activity is that the latter is lacking in that concomitant reflex awareness of the self-in-act which marks the former: we know or feel or desire without being aware of the fact, or at least awareness is lacking to the extent to which the activity in question is in fact buried in the unconscious.

If then we are to admit the possibility of any apprehension at all at an unconscious level, it seems unreasonable to exclude ends and objectives from the type of reality that might be so apprehended. Indeed the preservation of self-esteem or the avoidance of conflict or other similar motives which account for the exclusion of so much psychic activity from the clear light of consciousness might be expected to exert a particularly powerful repressive influence where ends and objectives are concerned.

If this is so, we are forced to make a distinction between objectives at which we aim and which are known to us in such a way that we are clearly aware of that knowledge, and other objectives which are apprehended unconsciously. We are moreover forced to admit unconscious ends as ends in the proper sense of the word if the whole argument, familiar to us in the treatise *de fine*, the argument concerning the concatenation of ends in human activity, is not to become meaningless. Ends are divided into immediate, remote and ultimate; all immediate ends are in the last resort related to some ultimate end and are undesirable therefore not in themselves but because of something which lies beyond them. The remote or ultimate end in fact explains the desirability of the immediate end; and in the case of unconscious motivations it is the end which is not consciously apprehended which does in fact explain the desirability of the consciously apprehended immediate end.

We need do no more than glance at the common experience of every man to assure ourselves that our more remote ends not uncommonly lie outside our direct awareness. Ask a man about his immediate objective in what he is doing and you may well be given a clear and satisfying answer : 'I am going to have dinner, to play golf; I am making a table, composing a song.' Ask him about the more remote purposes of his activities and you are likely to receive an answer which is at best vague and hesitant.

This is admitted by St. Thomas, who nevertheless found no difficulty in seeing these objectives, not consciously adverted to, as true ends motivating human actions and explaining by the attraction they exert the desirability of more immediate and more obvious goals. Indeed the supposition that only ends to which we consciously advert can be ends in the proper philosophical sense makes nonsense of the whole discussion of purpose and motivation with which we preface our moral theology, and divorces our speculation from the world of fact and reality. Nothing is more obvious than the complexity of our motivations in some of our simplest actions, and anyone who imagines that they can be readily analyzed and reduced to neat little formulae, with A desired on account of B, and B on account of C, C on account of D, and so forth, with everything snug and tidily fitting and certain, must be blind to the actual complexities of human motivation.

In the *Summa Theologica* St. Thomas deals with ends of which we are only *virtually* aware.[1] He does not ask *why* the more remote end does not emerge into explicit consciousness; perhaps it is simply not adverted to, while being readily enough accessible to consciousness should the need arise. But there seems to be no reason why we should not apply his train of thought to cases where, owing to the existence of some obstacle, the more remote end might *not* be readily accessible to explicit conscious-

[1] I II q. 1, a 6, ad 3m.

ness. In other words there seems to be no reason why we should not admit the motivating influence of ends which are apprehended below the level of what we ordinarily think of as consciousness.

For, in replying to the objection that a man does many things without thought of his ultimate end, St. Thomas points out that though the man may not be actually thinking of his ultimate end, nevertheless the intending of that ultimate end is present at least virtually in all volition. Thus he sees intention as not necessarily involving an actual and explicit awareness of the end. An intention is said to be actual when there is actual thought of the end and will to attain it; but this does not necessarily mean that the intention must be absolutely explicit: one could for instance while willing A be vaguely aware that A was a means to another end B—in which case in the willing of A there would be an actual though largely implicit willing of B. Indeed, as we have seen, experience shows clearly enough how rarely our motivations appear absolutely fully and explicitly in consciousness. Moreover, as was suggested above, an actual intention need not mean that the agent must recognize his actual intention in explicit self-consciousness, must be aware of his awareness of it. It is easy to will and not notice one's willing; to know and not reflect on one's knowing. In abnormal psychological conditions, dissociation can be so complete as to make it very difficult to bring the knowledge to light at all; and it seems impossible to avoid considering such abnormal phenomena as anything but exaggerations of phenomena which are quite normal. We all know—as the ascetical writers have all known so well—how readily we hide or dissimulate our true motives when they are such as to wound our self-esteem: in other words we are all familiar with the phenomenon of rationalization—though admittedly we are more likely in practice to recognize its presence in others than in ourselves.

Now one is not arguing simply that actual intention does not involve reflex knowledge; one is arguing that it need not involve a reflex knowledge which is perfect and absolutely clear to consciousness. For if our motivations were wholly outside consciousness, the admonitions of the spiritual writers that we should scrutinize our motives would be meaningless: we can scrutinize only those things which in some way or another lie within our consciousness. Moreover, if we had no knowledge at all of our motivations, we should not be masters of our own actions, and the actions themselves would not be true *actus humani*. In some sense or other these motivations must lie within our consciousness, not merely as *cognoscibilia* but as *actu cognita*. But they may be, and often are, known very obscurely—and with an obscurity which may be more or less voluntarily assumed or, if not voluntarily assumed, may yet be subject to some sort of voluntary control inasmuch as it is not impenetrable, for evidences of the unconscious motivation do appear in consciousness and so can lead back to their source.

Nor should it be supposed for a moment that to argue thus is to put forward some new theory in defiance of the Christian moral tradition. On the contrary, as we have already seen, it is the common and often repeated conviction of the ascetical writers through the ages that human beings are all too apt to allow their behaviour to be determined by motives quite other than those they think to be operative; and unless that assumption is accepted all the warnings of the ascetical writers against self-deception become meaningless. The author of the *Imitation* tells us: *Saepe male agimus, et peius excusamus. Passione interdum movemur et zelum putamus*: 'Often what we do is wrong, but our excuses for doing it are worse. Sometimes we are moved by passion but call it zeal.' And a host of other spiritual writers say the same thing in one way or another. For indeed no one has been more alive than they to the very real danger of self-deception and rationalization in the context of human motivations in general and the moral virtues in particular.

This leads us to the question of 'pseudo-virtues' (and, in the next chapter, of 'pseudo-vices'). It is not difficult to think of at least hypothetical examples. X practices severe bodily mortification : is his motive the love of God, the desire to share in Christ's sufferings, the need to master the unruliness of the flesh, or is it an unacknowledged, perhaps unsuspected, masochism ? (Flagellation figures in history, now as a canonical penance imposed by the Church, now as a medical remedy for frigidity or insanity imposed by doctors; we read of it as a self-imposed mortification in many saints' lives and as a sexual anomaly in many case-histories : it is not always easy to judge whether the supposed motivation was the real one, or whether more than one motive was operative.) Y is praised for his sexual continence and love of chastity; but is his continence merely a question of frigidity or inhibition, his chastity merely negative ? Z is reputed to have the childlike simplicity and meekness which the Gospel demands of us; but are these qualities merely the fruit of religious infantilism ? Such questions may in individual cases be all but impossible to answer with any certainty; in general it is undeniable that the 'penance' of the masochist is something very different from the penance of the saint; that the continence of the sexually inhibited has little to do with the positive and creative concept of Christian chastity; and that 'little ways' as practised by the saints may too easily degenerate into infantilism when practised by less exalted, and psychologically less stable, souls.

The business of the moral life then includes the careful scrutiny of motives; and that scrutiny in its turn must include the attempt to bring to light motivations which are true ends but which lead not to true religion and morality but to false.

Let us take the example of a man whose life is free of sexual sin but who is not troubled—being, in fact, repelled —by sexual stimuli : is his abstention from sexual indulgence true virtue or pseudo-virtue? Morality is a question not just of objective standards but of subjective responsibility and guilt or merit; if we speak of someone as a highly 'moral' person we mean not just that he (objectively) keeps the rules but that he is a good man, that his actions are the expression of good and praiseworthy motives—for the thing of ultimate importance in questions of human conduct and human destiny is not the right but the good. Everything then depends on motive: the three traditional determinants of good conduct are end, object and circumstances, and according to that traditional doctrine an action which is good in itself may become bad because its motive or end is bad.

If I refrain from actions hostile to others because of a deep-rooted timidity in myself, because I am afraid to cross swords with anyone even when it is my duty to do so, then the mere fact of abstention from hostile actions is no proof of virtue in me. (True, I can rejoice that this disinclination helps me on balance to lead a more charitable life than would be the case were I of a bellicose disposition, and so I can to some extent integrate my diffidence into the framework of the virtuous life and there may thus in the end be something of virtue in my pacific disposition.) Similarly with the sexually abstinent man, the whole question is *why* he abstains from sexual activity. It might be because it would involve obligations, duties, responsibilities which would be repugnant to his selfishness; it might be because he is acquiescing in a radically diseased attitude of mind towards sex, because he is hating and repudiating something good, something created by God; it might be that his soaring pride and vanity make him determined to see himself as a great ascetic, liberated from all the basic—and, to him, base—urges of the common man.

Yet he does in fact refrain from sexual sin, and that surely is continence, and continence is a true virtue? No, mere physical abstention does *not* necessarily mean continence in the theological sense.[2] It is far too readily assumed that the mere absence of some positive sinful act against a virtue implies the possession and practice of that virtue. That is not the case. Let us suppose that the man in question is married; he finds sexual activity repugnant to him; he abstains therefore from any extra-marital entanglements but he also abstains from the sexual intercourse which is not only licit for him but incumbent upon him in his married state. Here it is quite obvious that his abstention from sexual vagaries is motivated not by any love of the virtue of chastity but by a non-virtuous horror of sex. Or again, suppose a thief, a man who has it in his heart to steal when occasion offers, but who on this or that occasion refrains from theft because of the danger of detection, of trouble with the police, or because some other even less creditable purpose will be better served by abstention from theft: it is obvious again that his abstention is not motivated by the love of justice and therefore is not an act of the virtue of justice.

To make the point yet clearer let us pass on from these

[2] Definition of terms is perhaps advisable, as the terms are so often misunderstood or misapplied. Chastity is often taken nowadays to mean total abstention from sexual pleasure, which would make the Christian concept of chastity-in-married-life a contradiction in terms. For St. Thomas chastity means, not the abolition or atrophy of the sexual powers but their *control* by man's higher powers; continence, he notes, is used in two senses: first, as meaning abstention from all sexual pleasure for the sake of some praiseworthy end, and in this sense he regards it as a virtue; secondly as meaning the resistance of the mind to evil desires when they are vehement in a man, and this he regards as not attaining to the perfect nature of a moral virtue ('by which the sensitive appetite is so subject to reason that vehement passions contrary to reason do not arise in it') but as having in it something of virtue, being compared to *temperantia* as imperfect to perfect. (cf. *Sum. Theol.* II ii, cli & clv.) Here we are concerned with continence in the former sense, but again the whole question for us hangs on the phrase 'for some praiseworthy end'.

examples of abstention from actions which are evil to one in which it is a question rather of actions which are in themselves good. Suppose a man in whom the power-drive, the need to impress others, is very strong and deeply rooted. This urge may well be satisfied in the vigorous prosecution of activities which in themselves are wholly respectable. As a citizen the man will be prominent in all the committees, movements, drives, the object of which is the betterment of the life of the city; as a Catholic he will be a leading light in all the guilds and confraternities and in general all the good works of parochial life. But when he is thus achieving some great thing for his city or for the Church, is it civic virtue or love of the Church which moves him or is it the gratification of his power-drive and his lust for self aggrandisement? (It was said of Judas that his ostensible solicitude for the poor when he rebuked the extravagance of Mary Magdalen was not in fact any love of the poor but simply the fact that 'he was a thief'.) Clearly, until we have sorted out the man's motives and shown that the satisfaction of his power-drive is in fact subordinated to the end of civic virtue or love of the Church we cannot say that his action is virtuous action : it may spring not from virtue but from something quite different.

We cannot then simply assume that sexual abstinence though due to some traumatic childhood experience, some obsessive disgust, is nevertheless real continence, real virtue. It cannot be, if the abstention is simply due to disgust and nothing else. And indeed if, as is sometimes the case, a person is so conditioned by some traumatic experience that he is incapable, physically or psychologically, of sexual reactions and responses, then there is some question, to say the least, of the propriety of speaking of a virtue : in the circumstances he is *determinatus ad unum*, determined to one course of behaviour, and where there is *determinatio ad unum* there would seem to be no play of freedom and therefore no room for a moral habit.

There are plenty of traditional examples of the same sort of thing in other contexts : the almsgiving which is motivated by vanity, the cruel and crushing treatment of others which is motivated by hostility : here the ostensible motives, the motives to which the conscious mind of the agent will lay claim, will be charity, mercy, and so on in the first case, and the victim's need of training, discipline, the acquiring of humility and so on in the latter. But if these are not the real motives they cannot determine the character of the real behaviour : it will be vanity and enmity which do that; and since these are evil they render the action to that extent evil, though, as we have already seen, even such actions can to some extent be integrated into the life of charity.

Once admit then the legitimacy of the concept of a real end which does not emerge into consciousness or at least is not readily accessible to consciousness, and we are bound to admit the possibility of pseudo-virtue.

This is not to suggest that human freedom is an impossibility; on the contrary it is assumed as a fact. There is no question of putting forward a purely determinist theory of morality. Nor again is one unaware of the objection which might be brought against the theory of pseudo-virtues on a more practical level. 'If what you say is true,' it might be argued, 'you must mean that a man can never know where he stands so far as morality is concerned; and that is to rob him of all confidence in his good intentions, if not indeed to cause him to lose all respect for virtue in general and to adopt a cynical attitude of mind toward the whole idea of doing or being anything good.' No, there is no question of attempting to place any additional burden on the individual conscience or to induce in the individual a mood of hopelessness or cynicism. The argument does no more than the ascetical writers have always done with their warnings against self deceptions, their *hoc enim fecit et Crates philosophus* and their 'foolish virgins'; it does not suggest that *more* self-examination is needed, for too much introspection is as bad as too little, but simply that in the self-scrutiny which any ordinary Christian life demands, the importance of motivation which is more or less unconscious should not be overlooked. It must moreover be made quite clear that to describe behaviour which seems to spring from the virtue of justice or chastity as being in fact a question of pseudo-justice or pseudo-chastity is not to say that the person concerned, the agent, is a 'pseudo-person' or a wicked person. Precisely because his motivations lie outside his awareness, his behaviour may be (subjectively speaking) virtuous or perhaps morally insignificant—mere *actus hominis* as opposed to the deliberate and imputable *actus humanus*. Presumably we are all of us often unconscious of our true motives; that does not make us 'false' people. The man who generally speaking tries to do the objectively right thing, and who by and large tries to ensure that there is love and not hatred, contempt, selfishness, behind his activity, is certainly not to be regarded as a 'false' person. The falsity in the examples we have been considering lies simply in the ascription of this or that action to this or that virtue when in fact it springs not from the virtue but from something quite different. But it is obviously a good thing for us to be on our guard against making such ascriptions about ourselves and perhaps becoming smugly convinced that we are truly just, generous, chaste, humble, when in fact we are not. And facile and superficial ascriptions of that sort can be dangerous not only to an individual but in the end to a society as well.

In the world at large as we know it there are certain psychological phenomena with which we are all too familiar: the unacknowledged frustration which induces a virulently hostile and disapproving attitude toward the thing desired but not possessed; the guilt-sense which must find a scapegoat on which to project the intolerable burden; the frustrated power-drive which finds a poor substitute for greatness in some form of tin-pot tyranny; the thwarted pleasure-drive which consoles itself by making life as unpleasant as possible for other people; the inferiority complex which can brook no criticism. It would be foolish indeed to suppose that these things, so commonly met with in human affairs generally, were never to be met with amongst ourselves inside the Church; and we do well to be on the alert for manifestations of them in the particular coinage of modern Catholicism. If I find myself attacking something in the name of virtue with an emotional virulence not rationally warranted, or expending all my time and energy in bringing every contemporary evil to the door of some particular scapegoat; if I find I have really no time to be pro-anything because I am too busy being anti-something; if, being in a position of authority, I find that I try to rule my subordinates with a Stalinesque rigidity and a refusal to let them do any thinking for themselves; if I find myself becoming a Grundy, always desperately engaged in discovering a mortal sin in every peccadillo; finally, if I find myself as a Catholic so much on the defensive that I regard any criticism of life within the Church as a blasphemy and a falsehood, every bad Pope maligned, every evil chapter in Church history an invention of the Church's enemies; if I find any of these things happening, then I have good grounds for suspecting that these are cases in which unacknowledged drives are powerfully operative and in sad need of being brought to light.

But it cannot for a moment be agreed that the situation of the individual as here depicted is a hopeless one; on the contrary, for while the content of the unconscious may be difficult of access it cannot normally be said to be wholly inaccessible, nor indeed have the ascetical writers regarded it as such. We might here recall the words of Christ: 'Not everyone that saith to me, Lord, Lord, shall enter into the kingdom of heaven: but he that doeth the will of my Father.'[3] Motives are to be tested, in the last resort, not by the words one may use, not even by words

[3] *Matt.* vii, 21.

of the conscious mind, but by whether in general, in all contexts, the will of God is loved and done. And in fact if a man who exerts authority cruelly does so out of hatred and enmity, though he explains his conduct to himself —and perhaps to others—in terms of the most virtuous motives, his true motives, his defect of intention, will be likely to appear somehow on the surface in such a way that it can be made accessible to consciousness—to his own in the end as it certainly will be more immediately to everyone else's. In the process of analysis or psychiatric treatment it is the normal procedure to bring to light intentions which are inherent in what a man actually does; while, therefore, it may sometimes be difficult to know one's own motives, it cannot be said to be normally impossible for something to be brought directly or indirectly into the light of consciousness which will enable a man to know what really drives him.

On the other hand one is certainly not claiming—nor do any of the spiritual writers—that it is an easy thing to know for certain of what spirit we are. But this once again is no cause for despair; it ought on the contrary to be the foundation of a humble trust in God. If morality were in fact based on a conviction of one's own certain knowledge of one's own righteousness, it would indeed be a pseudo-morality as far as Christian standards are concerned; for as Christians 'our sufficiency is from God'. For here again, as in questions of objective morality, the demon of neat and tidy labellings rears his ugly head: we want to know just where we stand; we must have a clear and distinct idea of our guilts and our merits; we must know on what precise rung of the mystical ladder we are poised. And all that is as un-Christian as it is foolish and otiose. It is foolish *because* it is otiose; and it is otiose because the questions are not answerable in that sort of way; but it is un-Christian because it is putting the accent on the wrong places: between the sheer passivity of quietism and the sheer activism of a self-achieved self-righteousness there lies the fundamental Christian attitude : Our Lady's 'He that is mighty hath done great things in me', St. Paul's 'Christ liveth in me', or the cry of St. Teresa, asking what she must do not to undo the works of God in her soul, and the lament of the mystic Marguérite d'Arbouze: 'I spoil everything.' Christian confidence is not based on a clear and distinct apprehension or righteousness of conduct or motive, luckily for most of us, for it is not self-confidence but Christ-confidence : and the Publican in the Temple is a figure not of despair or diffidence but of undying hope. Moreover we should not forget, or be misled by the same demon of neat tabulation into ignoring, the complexity of human motivations, a complexity which makes it possible for the same action to issue from good motives and bad motives at the same time. A man could be filled with charity, a charity which would colour his behaviour as a whole, and yet at the same time he could be driven by some of the undesirable unconscious motives we have been considering : they would spoil the perfection of his activity, they would not altogether destroy its goodness. The deformity would remain : the almsgiving would not be true almsgiving, nor the chastity true chastity; they would be pseudo-virtues, they would lack the full reality of these virtues as such to the extent that they were determined by vanity or some other unworthy motive; but they would not in the last resort be wholly without value because to the extent to which there was goodness in their motivation they would have in them the value of true virtue and the love of God.

9. THE PROBLEM OF PSEUDO-VICE

In the last chapter it was suggested that in given cases a right action or behaviour pattern may, because of unconscious or unnoticed motivations, be lacking in the moral goodness of the virtue concerned. We have now to consider whether it is not equally possible for an objectively wrong action or behaviour pattern to be subjectively speaking either wholly or at least in great measure guiltless; not that an unconscious motive however good can turn an objectively vicious action into a good one, but that a vicious habit which is involuntary (in the sense to be explained in a moment) can so obscure the judgement and fetter the will that the agent is not in fact capable in the circumstances of what theologians regard as a perfect human act, that is, an action that is wholly free and therefore responsible.

The distinction between objective standards of morality and subjective degrees of imputability, and the possibility of their failing to coincide in given cases, is again at the root of the matter. A legalistically-trained Christian can find this difficult to understand. It says in the catechism or the moral textbooks (he will argue) that this action is a mortal sin : but I have done this action, therefore I am in mortal sin. Yet the same catechism and textbooks make it plain that no action can be a grave sin unless the agent is fully conscious of what he is doing, fully aware of the gravity of it, and does what he does quite freely and deliberately; and the traditional doctrine of responsibility enumerates the *hos voluntarii*, the physical or psychological conditions which destroy or diminish the freedom of action and therefore the responsibility of the agent: ignorance, physical compulsion, fear, passion, habit, pathological states.

The relevance of some of these is clear enough. If a man does a wrong action thinking it to be right, the action—provided his ignorance is not his own fault—is not sinful. If he is physically forced to do a wrong action he cannot be held responsible for it; if he acts wrongly under the influence of terror he is at most partially to blame; in the same way if a gust of passion (for which he is not morally to blame) sweeps him off his feet he is to be regarded either as not responsible for what he does or at least as not fully responsible. But the last two factors mentioned in the list are more complicated; and it is these that we must consider in detail here.

A habit as here understood means simply a propensity to act in a given way caused by the frequent repetition of such activity in the past. A man who has trained himself to act generously or bravely will tend always so to act; a man who has got into the habit of over-eating, will tend to over-eat always. Now some habits can be said to be so mechanical as to be wholly involuntary: physical mannerisms would come into this category, but so also would some habits which objectively speaking are morally bad, as when a child whose parents are always using blasphemous language picks up such language, without deliberation or even comprehension, and begins automatically to use it. But generally speaking an acquired vice or virtue means a propensity to a form of *deliberate* action: we acquire a fondness, a predisposition, for this or that form of action, and therefore we *tend* to indulge in it, and normally, when we do, the action flows both from the habit and from the deliberate will to indulge it. But a moral habit can often be not a simple but an extremely complex thing; morally speaking, a lot will depend on the psychological genesis of the habit, and it is this that we have to consider.

Let us note, first, that the Church continues to hold that normally a man must be held to be free and therefore

accountable for his actions : it will not sanction the contemporary tendency to think that there is *never* anything
morally blameworthy in crime, that it is *always* a question
simply of some psychological disability, and that the same
is roughly true also of sin. Pope Pius XII, for instance,
declared erroneous the view that sexual lapses in adolescence are to be regarded as 'not worthy of serious notice'
since 'as a general rule passion destroys the freedom
needed for an act to be morally imputable';[1] and opposed a prevalent tendency to deny all responsibility in
criminal acts by affirming that man is 'not a thing, not an
automaton whose functioning would depend on some in-
animate mechanism; nor even a mere combination of
feelings and impulses which would pass over into act
only under the effect of instinct and appetite'; 'in virtue
of his natural faculties' man 'enjoys the capacity of self-
determination and must consequently be considered responsible for his self-determined acts, at least until the
contrary is proved or until there is a well-founded
doubt'.[2]

The *norm* therefore is freedom; and responsibility
must be presumed unless there is at least a well-founded
doubt to the contrary. In practice such doubts do, not
infrequently, arise. In an interesting discussion of the
problem of responsibility in *Theological Studies* in 1956,
Fr. J. Lynch, s.j. refers to a matrimonial nullity suit which
was tried by the Roman ecclesiastical court in 1941 and
in which 'the validity of matrimonial consent was at-
tacked on the ground that the man, though manifestly
intelligent, was afflicted with "constitutional immorality"
which made it impossible for him to evaluate sufficiently
the ethical side of the marriage act'; the court eventually
refused, for lack of evidence, to declare the marriage null,
but not before one of the presiding judges had stated as a

---

[1] cf. *Acta Apost, Sedis*, XLIV, April 12, 1952.
[2] cf. 'Notes on Moral Theology', *Journal of Theological Studies*,
June 1956, pp. 168–9.

matter of principle that 'it is not enough for freedom and imputability that there be a mere conceptual cognition; there is required in addition the ability to weigh and evaluate the substantial elements of the proposed action.' Fr. Lynch goes on to discuss further this notion of 'evaluative' knowledge which, though 'no novelty in moral theology' may be 'so taken for granted that some of its practical applications are overlooked'. A small child may have learnt to distinguish between good and evil and to describe certain actions correctly as good or bad, 'but we would hesitate to say that the child appreciates the real significance of goodness and badness, that he has a full realization of their moral implications': the growth of the evaluative concept is gradual, and one cannot think of the child 'as guilty of real sin', for the lack of evaluation of 'the meaning behind the concept of sin, while it need not in any way affect the freedom of the physical act, quite definitely affects its imputability as a morally culpable act. Knowledge requisite for subjective sin involves something substantially more than the ability to identify an act as sinful.'

The author goes on to apply the same reasoning to forms of adult behaviour, and takes the example of a man acting under the influence of alcohol. 'All moralists admit the responsibility for sinful acts committed in such circumstances may be diminished to varying degrees. And yet many a person under the influence is still able to recognize a contemplated act as sinful. The fact of its being sinful, however, no longer makes any impression on him, or makes far less impression than it ordinarily would.' Now it must be noted that in a court of law, in cases such as the one referred to above, a lack of responsibility must be proved, established beyond doubt; but the same is not true of a purely private assessment of responsibility, either by an individual searching his own conscience or by a confessor: there, it would seem, a 'well-founded doubt' is sufficient to work on.

The task of the confessor, as we have seen, is to send

the penitent away in *peace*, to help him acquire a *creative* attitude to morality, building up a positive resistance to evil, a longing for—and ultimately a connaturality with —all forms of goodness. In countless cases this means in practice having to combat the *depressive* effect of a continuous and apparently fruitless fight against some ingrained evil habit. What is the confessor to do?

The first thing is to recognize, as of supreme practical importance, the *complexity* of many moral habits. Often they are a question, not just of a simple inclination or liking, as when we say of a man that he is 'keen' on tennis or playing the flute, but of a modification both of mental processes and of emotional drives. The habit of heavy drinking is a case in point. We can say of a man that he likes having a drink about six o'clock and so has formed a habit of doing so; but what of the compulsive or obsessive drinker? Some experts hold that among those for whom alcohol is a problem the number of 'pure' alcoholics is very small; most are driven to drinking (and it might equally well be drugs or something else of the sort) simply—whether they recognize the fact or not—as an escape from some intolerable situation. Certainly this is true of many drinkers; and it shows, incidentally, the folly of the kind of 'cure' which deals with the symptom while blandly leaving untouched the underlying cause of the symptom: it is of little use to stop the patient's drinking if he is merely driven to look for some other, perhaps more harmful, form of escape. The compulsive drinker's mental attitude and emotional response to alcohol are quite different from those of the normal drinker: for him it means a relief from inner panic: emotionally he is in fact driven by an anxiety amounting to panic; his thinking (with regard to this particular problem) becomes muddled and his panic-fear becomes an overwhelming passion. He is driven not by a simple desire for pleasure but by a desire for relief from some deep insecurity or anxiety, a desire which is more or less beyond his rational control; radically therefore it is *ignorance* (muddled thinking) and *passion* which substantially influence his conduct and so affect his responsibility.

The same sort of thing can be true, to take another example, in cases of habitual indulgence in solitary sexual practices, for here too the dominant motivating factor may be not the simple desire for pleasure but the need to escape from an intolerable anxiety, panic or misery; such practices often begin at a very early age, long before any understanding of them—and *a fortiori* of the moral issues involved—is possible, and it is difficult to say at what precise age and point of mental development the necessary 'evaluative' knowledge and consent can be said to come fully into play; finally, here more than anywhere else we must reckon with the depressive effect of endlessly fighting what seems to be a hopelessly losing battle, and a battle in which setbacks are particularly conducive to feelings of shame, self-depreciation, inferiority, anxiety.

A great deal of real and quite unnecessary anguish of spirit could be avoided if the principles we are considering were common knowledge among ordinary Christians, but they are not; the tragic fact is that many really good and devout people are driven almost to despair because, battling ineffectually with a habit which in fact is largely involuntary, they are convinced that every fall is a mortal sin and that therefore they are almost certainly doomed to perdition. Some theologians, while agreeing that such sins could not in the circumstances be mortal, have been opposed to the idea that the penitent should be told this, lest he be thereby lulled into a carefree and conscienceless acquiescence in the indulgence of his habit. This argument might still be held to apply to penitents who, though coming into the above category so far as habit is concerned, are already too cavalier about their failings (though even with them it would seem wiser—and more honest and truthful—to try to instil a sense of the horror of sin in general rather than labour to perpetuate what is in fact a false conscience about this sin in particular); but it certainly does not apply to the people mentioned above whose consciences are far from lacking in delicacy and who long and pray to be freed from the habit which obsesses them and destroys their peace of soul. In their case moral theology is greatly indebted to psychology for an understanding of their real needs and the best way of helping them. Psychologists have shown us that the question is not as simple as it was once thought to be, that it is not always and in all circumstances simply a matter of more and more effort and will power, and that on the contrary there are cases where an ever more intensive gritting of teeth will make matters not better but worse.

An obvious and extremely common example is that of adolescent masturbation.[3] A boy has contracted this habit, perhaps in quite early childhood long before he was capable of making any moral judgement about it; it has become deeply ingrained; but now he is determined to turn over a new leaf. The habit may in fact be due to some anxiety-state quite unconnected with sex, but he will be unaware of this; so, his resolution taken he grits his teeth, he bends all his efforts (and therefore his thoughts) to the conquering of the habit; he worries unceasingly about the danger of lapsing and, if he does lapse, is filled with remorse and with yet greater worry and anxiety. He is caught therefore in a vicious circle: the more he masturbates the more he worries and the more he worries the more he masturbates. He is going about the problem in exactly the wrong way; his incessant preoccupation with his problem, his constant gritting of teeth, his endless repetition of 'I won't, I won't', have the effect of keeping constantly before his imagination the very practices from which he is trying to escape and so of dooming his efforts to failure, for, as Baudouin's Law puts it, when the will and the imagination are in open conflict, the imagination always wins.

Here again therefore the first essential step is to try to

[3] cf. *supra*, chapter 7.

straighten out muddled thinking and to cope with the *cause*—worry, depression, anxiety-state—of which the masturbation is often, in such cases, but a symptom. It may be necessary to convince the boy that his difficulties do not brand him either as a psychological or physiological oddity or as a monster of iniquity. (To threaten with hell-fire a boy who is struggling manfully with his difficulties is as pernicious and dangerous—and ignoble—as was the old technique of threatening dire diseases and insanity; moreover it has to be borne in mind that a boy who has a real sense of God and of the stuff of the moral life may well have a deep if obscure awareness of the distinction between objective moral standards and subjective degrees of responsibility and guilt, and ill-informed and unrealistic fulminations may well strike him precisely as unrealistic and so serve not to help him conquer his failings but to undermine his faith in the objective standards themselves as propounded to him, through its representatives, by the Church.) He needs on the contrary to be shown how his physical urges as such are a natural and inescapable part of the general process of physical growth; how they come upon him in fact before he is psychologically equipped to see them and therefore to react emotionally to them in fully human and not just physiological terms; he needs to be shown how to cope with his anxieties and worries if it is these that lie at the root of his troubles, and how to keep his imagination and his whole personality healthily and creatively occupied.

But what of such habits when they continue into later life, and in general of adult habits which seem to be compulsive? Sometimes a habit in a given individual can be said to be clearly and certainly obsessive: one thinks for instance of kleptomania or severe cases of scrupulosity. The question here is not whether the sufferer can be guilty of mortal sin within the sphere of his obsession, but whether he is to be *told* that he cannot. The answer seems certainly to be yes: first because this is the only honest course for confessor or director to pursue, but secondly because it is the only way that is likely to prove of therapeutic value. This has been clearly and cogently stated by Fr. Joseph Nuttin in his *Psychoanalysis and Personality*.[4] 'Many of the problems which present themselves to the patient[5] as *moral* ones,' he writes, 'are fundamentally not moral but *psychological*.' And he takes as illustration first the problem of scrupulosity, which we shall consider in a moment, and then the problem of obsessive masturbation. Of this latter he writes : 'the therapist should not directly help the patient to overcome the tendency to masturbation. Even for the psychiatrist who looks upon therapeutic treatment, not only as a means of psychic equilibrium, but as a renewal of the moral and spiritual personality, the solution will not consist simply in reducing the number of pollutions, but in *remedying the patient's psycho-asthenic dispositions* as a whole, and thus freeing him from all his obsessional ideas.' And he goes on to state emphatically that 'an important part of the treatment', here as with scruples, is 'to *detach* the patient *emotionally* from the kinds of behaviour in question, and especially to *relax his moral attitude towards them*. He would then come to realize that his scrupulosity or his tendency to masturbation is no more than a *form of psychological reaction*, and quite a different thing from sin. Often the pathological reaction will disappear as the moral aspect of the conduct ceases to be an obsession ; the moral preoccupation being simply one aspect of a psycho-pathological symptom.'

This whole argument may seem (and has seemed) to some to be imprudent and even subversive; but it has to be asked whether the imprudence does not lie rather in rejecting it out of hand. For if, instead of trying to bring about the emotional detachment and the relaxing of the moral attitude here advocated, we continue simply to

[4] pp. 142–3.
[5] For 'patient' we can read here, for this immediate context, 'penitent'.

drum into the sinner the idea of the heinousness of his sin
and the completeness of his own responsibility for it, we
are doing our best to ensure that his life shall be a misery,
a continuous agony of spirit; we are also being dishonest,
but more than that, we are running a very grave risk of
driving a truly good and God-loving person to despair, a
despair for which there is not the slightest warrant.

The prudent course is surely to help the penitent to see
his problem in its true perspective and to be quite clear
about the principles involved. And he will be unable to do
either of these things unless he can achieve the emotional
detachment of which Fr. Nuttin speaks. If he is emotionally overwhelmed by his problem it will fill the whole of
his moral horizon : wholly absorbed in his conflict with
what by hypothesis is his pseudo-vice, he will have no
time or energy to give to the extirpation of any real vices
with which he may be burdened or to the growth in virtue
generally and in the love of God. This is particularly obvious in the problem of scrupulosity. The symptoms are
all too readily recognizable : the endless and quite abor-
tive worrying— Was it a mortal sin or not ? ; the fretting
over the imagined incompleteness of past confessions or
the inadequacy of contrition; the inability to accept the
judgement of the confessor, and consequently the restless
and sometimes frenzied running from one confessor to
another; the compulsion felt during confession to go into
endless irrelevant detail for fear of 'leaving something
out' . . . There is no doubt whatsoever that this problem
is 'fundamentally not moral but psychological'. 'The
scrupulous patient,' writes Fr. Nuttin, 'who never stops
scrutinizing his behaviour for its hidden guilt, does not
fundamentally present any moral problem at all. We do
not mean that such a way of behaviour is not really culpable—on that point we pass no judgement—but we mean
that the apparently moral attitude that dominates his way
of looking at everything he does is *not* fundamentally a
moral attitude at all; it is probably a purely *psychological*
attitude towards himself. This attitude can often be the

result of a longing to outshine others, manifesting itself in the pathological form of a desire for absolute perfection and purity, with scrupulosity as a mere sickly symptom of these desires and longings. The "moral" attitude of this kind of scrupulous individual is a psychological problem related to his thwarted longing to assert himself; and it is to this and not to the moral or non-moral aspect of his behaviour that the therapist's attention should be directed.'[6]

Long ago St. Alphonsus remarked that scruples often arise from pride;[7] but it must be emphasized again that it is at least likely to be a question of pride in a psychological rather than in a moral sense, in other words of unconscious perfectionism rather than of conscious indulgence in the capital vice; and the only hope of effective help for the scrupulous penitent lies in persuading him that his troubles are in fact psychological; that he must do all he can to achieve the emotional detachment and the relaxation of moral attitude considered above; and that as far as the subject-matter of his scruple is concerned he has every reason *not* to worry about his state of soul here and now or his happiness hereafter.

What in fact is the confessor to tell him? The fundamental principle is clearly stated by Prümmer: 'Since the judgement of the scrupulous is so perturbed that they are incapable of making any clear and certain judgement with regard to the subject-matter of their scruples, it follows that in this matter *they are incapable of grave sin,* since there cannot be grave sin without clear and certain knowledge.'[8]

Everything must start from this point: the penitent may be highly gifted intellectually, he may be cultured, learned, theologically well-informed—but in this particu-

[6] Nuttin, *ibid.*

[7] *Theol. Moral.* 1 i, n. 12; cf. Prümmer, *Manuale Theologiae Moralis,* t. i., p. 200.

[8] Prümmer, *op. cit.*, t. i., p. 201; (italics mine).

lar matter his gifts are of no avail since his fears are irrational; his first step then is to be humble enough to
accept this fact about himself, and simple and childlike
enough to accept the corollaries. Prümmer goes on to
say that the scrupulous person is excused both from the
duty of 'diligent examination of conscience' and from
the material integrity of confession[9]—and this is obvious
enough since both things imply judgement and of this he
is incapable. He must be convinced therefore that where
the subject-matter of his scrupulosity is concerned: (a)
he cannot sin gravely; (b) therefore he need never debar
himself from receiving communion because of an anxiety
about his sinfulness, nor on the other hand must he keep
going to confession either in order to go to communion
or from fear of being damned if he should die: it may
well be advisable for him to make his confessions rare
but regular, and to limit himself in them as was suggested
in an earlier chapter, to some simple, invariable and all-
inclusive formula which will cover any and all wrong-doing in the past including any defect of any kind in any
confession, even the one now being made.

The suggestion that confession should be rare but regular is based on two considerations: the regularity may
help to build up a resistance to his obsession by giving
him a feeling of stability and a regular renewal of his
(doubtless very shaky) feeling of confidence; the rare-
ness may prevent his aggravating his anxiety-state by constantly giving in to it, and is justified by the fact that
(where his scruples are concerned) he is never bound,
morally or legally, to go to confession at all.

This last point is perhaps worth emphasizing, since it
may well seem strange to a legalistically-trained modern
western Catholic. It is said that in eastern Catholicism and
the Orthodox Church scrupulosity is unknown and that

---

[9] i.e. the statement of the precise species (with any substantially
aggravating circumstances) and, as far as may be, the number, of
all grave sins.

the word has no equivalent; even in the west it is not until the later part of the Middle Ages, the age of the 'tech-
nicians' of morals, that it is seriously treated; thus, as one
writer (and sufferer) has put it: 'one would not be very
far from the truth if one asserted that the disease of scrupulosity was brought into existence as a result of the juridical element introduced by moral theologians in the
directives of the moral life.'[10] As the same writer goes
on to point out, 'the law exists, it must be taken into account; its existence is beneficial and one must be thank-
ful for it'—it 'canalized the religious stream of life' and in
so doing provided a safeguard against illuminism and
other aberrations of the religious impulse; but the fact
remains that 'the law is one thing, its interpretation quite
a different matter', and an interpretation which defeats
the end of the law is a misinterpretation, so that, where
the scrupulous are concerned, we may well ask with the
same author whether it is not permissible 'to wish that
the paralyzing strictures of legalism might be removed
from these sick souls, that the timid, craving for a freedom
which is too frequently forgotten, should be placed once
more in the full stream of the living waters of grace, for
these souls are so frequently held back and immobilized
by the theological asperities of canonical strictures which
were providentially established not to afflict weaklings
like them but to prevent the devastating flood of false
mysticism on the one hand and, on the other, stagnation
through quietist indolence.'[11]

But the 'living waters of grace' are above all the Eucharist, the practice of frequent and if possible daily
communion; and the scrupulous person must be encouraged to make this practice his own. He must be told,
gently, patiently, firmly, again and again, that his inhibit-

---

[10] cf. 'A Spiritual Cure for Scrupulosity', *Blackfriars* Nov. 1943, pp.
413 (tr. from an unsigned article in *La Vie Spirituelle*, vol. lii, suppl.
pp. 141 *sqq.*).
[11] *ibid.*

ing feeling of total, juridical unworthiness—we are all, of course, utterly unworthy, but that is another matter— is irrational, part of his malady, and not to be given in to; he must be reminded of his inability to commit grave sin in matters about which he is scrupulous; he must be reminded again and again therefore that he is free to receive communion, and ought to do so, no matter what he may feel about it.

The Church's law in this respect is often misunderstood. The Council of Trent laid it down that 'those who are conscious of being burdened by mortal sin (*quos conscientia peccati mortalis gravat*)' must confess their sins before receiving holy communion, 'however contrite they may think themselves to be'.[12] The Council does not require the communicant to be certain that he is free from grave sin and therefore in the 'state of grace': it requires only that he should *not* be conscious—and certain, for we can take *conscientia* as meaning *certa scientia*, certain knowledge[13]—of being in mortal sin. The distinction is vital: it means that the man who thinks he *may* have committed a mortal sin, or even that he *probably* has (provided the probability is not so overwhelming as to amount to moral certitude) is not excluded from receiving holy communion without previous confession: only the man who is *certain* he has committed mortal sin is so debarred. Scrupulous people will be reluctant to act on this: they will say, 'Yes, but suppose I really am in a state of sin, I shall commit a sacrilege'; but again the answer is clear: You cannot commit a sacrilege unless you are *certain* of being in a state of grave sin. The 'doubtful' or even 'probable' sinner who receives communion without previous confession is doing a good and virtuous action; more than that, if he were in fact in a state of mortal sin, the sin would be remitted by his reception of the holy Eucharist;

---

[12] *Sess.* xiii, *can.* ii, Denzinger. Bannwart, 893.
[13] cf. Merkelbach: *Theol. Moral.* t. iii, n. 271.

so far from his action being sacrilegious it would be virtuous, and so far from burdening his soul with further sin it
would cleanse it of the sin with which it was actually burdened.

It may be noted further that in the case we have just
been considering—the man who had in fact committed
mortal sin though he was not certain of the fact—he would
not even need to be contrite (in the technical sense of
the word[14]) for his reception of the Eucharist to be
worthy and fruitful. Perfect contrition is a prerequisite
only in the case of a man who is *certainly* in mortal sin
when he must celebrate Mass or must communicate and
a confessor is not available; here, 'attrition' is enough,
the attrition necessary for the worthy reception of any
sacrament. In other words, no more is required here in
the way of sorrow than is required for confession itself. Now a confessor would doubtless normally advise
and urge a man who thought himself to be probably in
a state of grave sin to confess before communicating,
though even in the case of a non-scrupulous person this
would be only advisable, not necessary; in the case of a
scrupulous person the confessor may well advise and urge
the contrary. In doing so he should make it clear to the
penitent that there is no question of any relaxation or di-
lution of the law; in acting on such advice, in not con-
fessing, the scrupulous penitent is *complying* with the
strict letter of the law.

We may note further that Prümmer is saying in effect
what was said above when he lays it down that when-
ever it is doubtful whether an action is voluntary and
therefore imputable or not, we should follow the principle that if the action is objectively wrong it should be
regarded as involuntary, if objectively right it should be
regarded as voluntary and free and therefore meritori-

---

[14] 'Contrition' is sorrow and repentance motivated by the supernatural love of God; 'attrition' is the effect of some other supernatural motive, such as the fear of damnation.

ous, the reason being that 'no one is to be regarded as wicked unless his wickedness is proven, and in such cases voluntary wickedness cannot in fact be proved, so that the confessor must be very gentle in judging them; on the other hand if the action in question is a good one there is no reason why it should not be taken as freely and voluntarily performed until the contrary is proved.'[15] The timid, scrupulous soul therefore, always afraid that his good actions have not been properly carried out or have been spoilt by some unworthy motivation or by his general sinfulness, must be gently but categorically and repeatedly told the opposite: No, these were good actions; your prayers, your communions, are good and will bring you great grace; your kindnesses, generosities, patience with others and with yourself, your own personal struggles too: all these are good, and should be a source for you of encouragement, thankfulness, joy.

It must be emphasized that if the foregoing considerations are valid they are valid only in general: they will need adaptation to each individual case; and always they are to be seen in the light of two fundamental facts: first, we cannot drive out devils by Beelzebub, cannot hope to cure a scrupulosity which at least seems to be closely connected with legalism and perhaps with a sort of practical pelagianism by imposing further burdens of impossible 'musts'; secondly, we shall do much harm if, because the penitent's fears are irrational, we treat them as non-existent or trivial or as 'a lot of nonsense', or if we treat the penitent himself as an imbecile or a mentally defective child instead of what he is, an adult burdened with a real and substantial problem which it is our business to help him to meet in an adult way. His sense of guilt is largely irrational; but we have to allow for and in a sense *respect* the irrational; indeed it may be helpful precisely to stress the fact that it need not be totally irrational or unreal. Even in irresponsible sin there

[15] Prümmer, *op. cit.*, t. i., p. 61.

can be sinfulness and therefore shame.[16] If we stress the idea of *freedom* (from mistaken 'musts' and sanctions and therefore from fears) and of being not outside the law but according to the strict letter of the law, and if at the same time we shift the emphasis from particular sins to general *sinfulness* (with shame as its rightful concomitant), then we may help the penitent towards eradicating what is unreal in his situation by integrating what is real in it.

Now these principles and this approach to practical moral difficulties would seem to apply not merely to cases which are clearly obsessive but in degree to others too where for one reason or another it is questionable how complete the voluntariness of actions is, how complete the agent's responsibility, his power to control his urges and drives. Often the confessor will find himself confronted by a penitent of whose sincerity and indeed fervour he can be in no doubt but who is plagued by some bad habit the history and circumstances of which will suggest, in the light of that sincerity, at least a large measure of compulsiveness and therefore perhaps a psychological rather than a moral problem, or at least a psychological as well as a moral problem. If this is so he will surely be well advised to follow the main lines of the policy advocated by Fr. Nuttin, trying to liberate the penitent from any 'psycho-asthenic dispositions' or 'obsessional ideas' which seem to be present in his behaviour and in part at least to determine it, trying also to 'detach' him emotionally from 'the kinds of behaviour in question, and especially to relax his moral attitude towards them' in so far as his moral attitude is in fact unhealthy, unrealistic and (as often happens) superstitious rather than religious in character. For *to the degree in which* his bad habit is in fact obsessive it will be not a vice but a pseudo-vice: he is then at most a 'dubious' sinner in this respect and so, as we have seen, he can be

[16] cf. Victor White, o.p.: 'Guilt', in *Christian Essays in Psychiatry*.

regarded as *not* a (grave) sinner and can be allowed, indeed encouraged, to regard himself in that light if this will bring about in him a necessary relaxation of tension or some other desirable result.

To say all this is far indeed from saying that the penitent should be encouraged to feel that he is 'outside the law' and can sin as he will with carefree impunity. This is no *pecca fortiter*, no incitement to a blithe abandonment of the commandments or to any false sense of security. (How wildly wide of the mark any such suggestion must seem to those who have had experience of the sufferings of such souls!) Emotional detachment, in the sense indicated, has nothing to do with irresponsibility; encouragement to achieve the former may sometimes need to go with prudent warnings against the latter. In some cases indeed it might be possible, perhaps advisable —but here we are on very debatable ground, and the suggestion, if valid at all, certainly presupposes an extremely careful and shrewd appraisal of character and temperament—to suggest to a penitent that *before* or at the onset of a temptation to his quasi-obsessive failing he should emphasize to himself—though without departing at all from the realities of his situation or from such 'emotional detachment' as he has managed to achieve —his own measure of freedom, responsibility, power of control, lest by believing that all control is out of the question he should end by losing such vestiges of control as he may actually have; whereas *afterwards*, if he has failed despite his good will, his care and his efforts, he should emphasize to himself his lack of complete freedom and responsibility, and refuse to be stampeded into thinking of what he has done as mortally sinful, as requiring prompt confession, or as an obstacle to receiving communion.

In dealing with this question of a bad habit which has been repudiated and against which the penitent is struggling but which he has not wholly conquered, Fr. L. L. McReavy suggests as a practical measure that the confessor should explain to the penitent 'in concrete terms, what, in view of his habit, is required for "full" deliberation and therefore for formal mortal sin. His frame of mind will more or less have to be : "I know this is gravely sinful, but I don't care, I'm going to do it." If, *post factum*, he can honestly say that this was not his frame of mind, he can reasonably assume that his relapse was not a formal mortal sin and can safely act accordingly.'[17] He cannot be assumed to have committed formal grave sin unless his attitude is 'I don't care': and this is just what the kind of penitent with whom we have been primarily concerned here does *not* say: his attitude is exactly the opposite: he cares deeply and sometimes desperately. Some penitents alternate between moods of caring deeply and moods (probably induced by depression over failures) of not-caring: perhaps these might be helped by the distinction suggested above between precedent sense of control and responsibility and subsequent emphasis on lack of control when in fact control is honestly felt to have been lacking.

The essential point remains : far too commonly the danger is the exact opposite of an incitement to irresponsibility. Many a good, devoted Christian, struggling painfully and perhaps heroically against overwhelming difficulties, may be led in the end to throw up the struggle as hopeless because, instead of being encouraged and above all enlightened as to the true nature morally speaking of the struggle itself and of his measure of responsibility, he has merely been told that he has free-will and must use it, that this or that action is a mortal sin (no distinction being made, still less carefully explained, between objective standards and subjective guilt), so that if he continues to commit this sin he is doomed. It is small wonder if, knowing by bitter experiences his inablity to avoid failures despite all his prayers and his efforts, he lives in constant fear, anxiety and discourage-

[17] cf. the *Clergy Review*, May, 1958, p. 299.

ment and may end in despair. How tragically far he is from leaving the confessional, as he should, 'in peace'!

The discussion of pseudo-virtues in the preceding chapter led to the practical conclusion that it is supremely important for us to open our eyes to ourselves and to discover so far as we can the real drives and urges which lead us to act as we do. The discussion of pseudo-vices also leads to an emphasis on the importance of knowing our true selves, but in the sense now of knowing and accepting our psychological limitations and therefore the limits of our moral responsibility, and using this knowledge and acceptance humbly, simply, creatively, first as part of the general process of accepting our dark shadow as a step towards becoming fully integrated personalities,[18] and then, in particular, as a means to a constant growth in and deepening of humility, to an awareness and acceptance of our total dependence on God and our inability to do anything for ourselves 'as of ourselves'. Thus, all the efforts, the struggle, perhaps the agony involved in such problems as we have been considering may not be in vain but on the contrary may lead in the end to great things : to the simplicity and lowliness without which true greatness is impossible, to the wisdom which has learnt where to look for real strength and stability and how to accept weakness with tranquillity, to a deeper understanding of and sympathy with the troubles of others, to an ability to carry our dark shadow, our cross, and not be carried, browbeaten, tyrannized over, by it. Finally, we become what it is the purpose of 'all the law and the prophets' to make us become—men and women filled, despite all difficulties and shortcomings, with faith and hope and trust, with generosity and devotedness to God and men, and above all with the love 'which is in Christ Jesus our Lord'.

[18] cf. my *The Paradise Tree*, chapter III.

10. THE VOCATION OF FAILURE

Can there be such a thing as having a vocation to choose the wrong vocation? A man adopts a career only to discover too late that it is the wrong career; he marries a woman only to find too late that she is the wrong woman; he settles down into a fixed, narrow groove only to find that at heart he is a wanderer. Perhaps we should see these errors of judgement as being no more than permitted by God; what is certain is that, the false situation once established, the frustration set up, the sufferer must surely see his vocation as being not at an end but at a beginning: something of value has to be made somehow out of the muddle.

There are of course many other types of frustration, and they are tragically common. There is the outwardly successful marriage which in reality has become empty of meaning: the husband and wife continuing—for the sake of appearances, or from a sense of duty, or because of the children—to act as a happy couple while in reality there is no longer any real communion between them or any hope of any. There are the men and women who long for married life but never achieve it. There are those who have a deep desire to become this or that, to achieve this or that, but have in the end to admit that they lack the necessary gifts. There are those who long for friends, and for companionship, but are condemned to loneliness. There are those who never seem to be able to make a real success of anything to which they put their hands. In the moral sphere there are those who long to make something worthy of their lives but who feel hopelessly defeated by some vice which they lack the ability to conquer; there are the cases of undeveloped conscience or deep character-defect where a vague desire to 'be good' is at times of emotional exaltation raised to grandiose heights of resolution only to be dashed again into the depths of despair when the next defeat occurs. And finally there is the frustration which weighs down all those whose faith, prayer, service of God, having begun with high ideals and generous self-giving and a deep sense of reality, seem to have become meaningless: faith no longer giving any assurance, any comfort, any drive; and prayer and God's service becoming a dull, empty routine, lacking any sense either of reality or of progress.

What are the normal human reactions to frustration? Milton gives us four types of reaction in his picture of the 'great consult' of the demons. Moloch stands for the way of blind rage: lashing out at something or other, ranting at this or that, quarrelling with one's friends, perpetually finding something to be indignant about and to attack. Belial on the other hand is for accepting the inevitable and hoping to become inured to it gradually and to forget: drowning one's sorrows, taking to drugs, trying not to think, sinking into a condition of life which at one time would have been unthinkable. Mammon's idea is to turn hell into a substitute heaven: if you cannot have the reality of life or love you can find or fashion some counterfeit; if you cannot have happiness you can concentrate on pleasure or power or prestige—

> *This desert soil*
> *Wants not her hidden lustre, gems and gold;*
> *Nor want we skill or art, from whence to raise*
> *Magnificence . . .*

Finally, Beelzebub, the realist: there is no escaping one's misery, and it is useless and senseless to try; but at least one can make others miserable too; at least that is better than

> *to sit in darkness here*
> *Hatching vain empires.*

These are all very human reactions; sometimes consciously and deliberately pursued, sometimes unconsciously. What ought the Christian reaction to be?

Certainly it ought not to be merely a passive resignation, a stoic endurance—which is more than likely to lead to an unconscious indulgence in one or other of the above reactions. There must be something more positive, more creative, than that. The folly of the cross, the wisdom of this world being folly to God: the fact is that often we just do not know what in the last resort is success and what is failure. What we do know is that superficial success can often have disastrous effects: the artist who becomes a fashionable painter and ceases to be an artist; the doctor who achieves fame and fortune at the expense of his integrity, and so on. Success can make us proud, slick, inhuman, cruel, superficial: perhaps then it is only failure that will save us? Everybody has a vocation to some form of life-work; but behind that and deeper than that, everybody has a vocation to be a person, to be fully and deeply a human being; and the second thing is more important than the first. It is more important to be a great person than to be a great butcher or baker or candlestick-maker; and if the only chance of achieving the first is to fail in the second the failure will be worth while, the world will be well lost. As M. Maritain has made so clear to us, the Church thrives not on 'rich means' but on poor; for it is these that chime with the folly of the cross.

What then is a man to do who finds himself in what might be called an environmental frustration: the wrong career or marriage, failure to achieve the work, the career, the life, desired? He is of course perfectly justified in adopting any good means—interests, friendships, hobbies—which will make life more bearable; but there must be more to it than that. If two people are deeply in love with each other and unable to marry it seems heartless to tell them to *use* the situation, creatively: yet in fact it is the one thing which can bring them any hope. Human relationships, we believe, are not confined to this world, they have an everlasting future; and if sorrow and frustration in this world will make the people concerned finer and deeper and capable in the end of giving each other a much richer and more wonderful love, they must surely be worth while. Pointing this out does not diminish the pain; but at least it shows a purpose in it.

And those whose marriages, whose careers, are a failure? They must accept what is at best a compromise, they must accept the mediocre: but will it not be worth while if it teaches them to be gentle with other failures, to be patient, to be greathearted? Happy, they might have been wrapped up in their own happiness and impatient of the sorrows of others; they might never have come to understand the human heart; they might have come to think of happiness and success as their due, and then, if their little world had collapsed through death or disaster, they would have had no resources.

Always we come back to the idea of sacrifice. We know intellectually that sacrifice is central to Christianity: it is quite another thing to see it as central to our own lives. But our Lord demands that every Christian take up his own cross—not Christ's cross but his own, the one determined by his own vocation in the deepest sense of the word—and follow in his footsteps: why? Because the inescapable pattern is that we reach life only through death, we come to the light only through the darkness: the grain of wheat must die, Jonah must be buried in the whale's belly.

But there is one type of case which demands special attention: the case of the Catholic—and especially the Catholic who neither marries on the one hand nor has a religious vocation on the other—who tries to do something for the faith (through writing, social work, or individual contacts of one sort or another) only to find that his good intentions are frustrated at every turn; is God repulsing him? On the contrary: the lesson there is surely that spiritual means are more powerful than ma-

terial ones; the work might have helped some, perhaps
many, but the loving acceptance of the frustration of
these ambitions will help far more. We believe in the
communion of saints. When we put a frustration of this
sort into the chalice of Christ's sacrifice we put in something of immense worth: the world will be saved by
failure.

But what of the cases of what could be called purely
personal frustration—the people for instance who seem
to be totally incapable of keeping the moral law? Perhaps the essential thing to tell them is that the idea of
being strong-willed or weak-willed is in a sense a misleading conception: that being strong-willed means in
fact having an over-ridingly powerful impulse to do or
achieve this or that; and that therefore they must concentrate simply on trying to love God. They must never
say, 'I shall never sin again'; they must on the contrary
expect to sin again and again, but they must not be ren-
dered desperate by their falls; they must try to live always with God (he did not despise the publicans and
sinners) in the hope that gradually they will come to
hate the wrong they do and so, gradually, escape from
it.

But also—and perhaps this is the main point—in a sense
it is not the escaping that is of most importance. We
know so much more nowadays of the extent to which
wrongdoing is determined. To exhort and require a defective personality to renounce all forms of frailty forth-
with and forever is necessarily to plunge him deeper and
deeper into despair; the essential thing is precisely to
help him to free himself from his sense of failure and to
give him a sense of achievement. First of all, pray, discover God, love God; your weaknesses need not stop
your doing that; on the contrary they can help you, for
it is the humble heart that finds God. At the same time of
course you must be trying to bring a little more order
into your moral life, but gently, little by little, being very
patient, not expecting a miracle, and always remember-

ing that this is secondary for you in importance; that the really important thing you are *achieving* more and more, day by day, is your prayer, your love, your closeness to God.

But how can one free oneself from a sense of failure? Only by accepting the failure with humility and humour, and turning it into greatness of soul. Some people are incapable of thinking of themselves as ever being a failure at anything, and so they never grow up. For in order to grow up we have first to grow down, down into the depths where we can not only see ourselves as we really are, but also laugh at ourselves in the midst of our tears. If we make morality solemn and pompous—the hushed voice, the worship of rectitude—we inevitably distort it; for it is human morality we are concerned with, and humanity, capable as it is of the sublime, is also still close to the monkey. If the fall makes us capable of horrible evil, still more it makes us foolish, feckless, feeble, ridiculous. We need what the missal calls the gift of tears, the deep sense of sin; but we also need the gift of laughter. To laugh at our failures as well as cry over them may well be the first step in the process of turning them into success. The delinquent boy has never learnt to laugh; perhaps, poor child, he has never had the chance. And any form of corrective regime, of character-training, of moral exhortation, which kills the laughter in people, kills also their chances of really emerging from failures and frailties into something which has about it a touch of greatness.

Tears, but never of self-pity; laughter, but never corrosive : these can help a man to take humbly to God the broken shards of failure, knowing that the divine creative and re-creative skill will not be lacking, or denied him. For a failure given to God ungrudgingly can be a form of that re-creative death of which St. Paul tells us : 'You know well enough that we who were taken up by Christ into his baptism have been taken up, all of us, into his

death. In our baptism we have been buried with him,
died like him, that so, just as Christ was raised up by his
Father's power from the dead, we too might live and
move in a new kind of existence.'

11. THE HUMAN PERSON

Man is a paradox, his life an unceasing tension between contradictories. Of fallen man this is true in the sense explained by Plato's horses and St. Paul's 'the flesh lusteth against the spirit'; but it is true in a yet more primitive sense of the human personality itself in its inner structure. Man is a paradox because being one thing, body-spirit, he is at the same time two things. He is a social animal, dependent physically, economically, culturally, spiritually upon society; he is a 'part of the universe', often at the mercy of natural forces, often determined not only in his behaviour but in his very way of thought by environment, upbringing, the history of the race, the history of the world. Against the might of the stars he is a puny invisible speck—it is not only the dead who are

> Roll'd round in earth's diurnal course
> With rocks, and stones, and trees.

Yet at the same time there is in the infinitesimal speck a sort of infinity; for Aristotle the spirit of man is 'in a manner all things'; for Christian theology it is *capax Dei*—made capable of union with the Infinite. This part of the universe is at the same time not part of the universe : the angels themselves cannot know a man's secret thoughts. The whirling speck of dust is at the same time 'the most perfect thing in nature'; the servant of the social and cosmic machines is the master for whose benefit they are made, and the country he inhabits is, in Kant's phrase, the 'kingdom of ends'.

The human person is traditionally defined as an individual self-subsistent substance of rational nature. Self-subsistent: by definition the person cannot inhere in another entity, as whiteness or rotundity in Socrates; nor enter into composition with another co-principle to form an entity, as material and spirit together make the nature of man. Individual; every human person, though sharing with other men a common human nature, is unique. The human person is not body-spirit merely, but *this* body and *this* spirit; the notion of person, says St. Thomas, adds individuating principles to the essence of man. We distinguish between individuating principles (*principia individualia*) and the principle of individuation (*principium individuationis*): the latter is the radical principle of numerical plurality of individuals in a species; the former are the formal principles of uniqueness in each individual as such. The modern use of the term 'personality' thus finds a justification from the Thomist point of view; and should save us from the error of regarding the human person purely *statically*—the temper of mind which did so much to bring decadent scholasticism into disrepute. The human person is the self-subsistent human individual, free and responsible master of his destiny and so forth. But at the same time he is *this* body and *this* spirit; a complexus of gifts, qualities, powers, which are his alone, the heir to hereditary influences, the material of a process of partly determined partly self-determined growth, which together make up this personality, this character or temperament, in distinction from all others. The personality in this sense is never static: it is always growing—or decaying: and every growth is a growth in its uniqueness, and therefore in its mystery. To know a human personality wholly we should have to know not only its physical uniqueness to the smallest detail but the entire content of its conscious mind, of its personal and collective unconscious heritage, its complexus of habits and tendencies, and the way in which its experience from moment to moment was acting upon, and being acted upon, by them. The heart of man is indeed, in Augustine's phrase, an abyss. Every man

therefore is a mystery : we can never know Socrates or
Tully simply by knowing human nature—a fact which
moralists do well to remember ; and the depths of this
uniqueness and mystery are inscrutable, except to the
eyes of God.

On the one hand, then, man is the servant of society :
his destiny as a social animal is to devote himself to the
common good, which is 'more divine' than his own particular good. On the other hand, having a supernatural
destiny and therefore a direct relationship with God, he
is that which society exists to serve : a society is fulfilling
its purpose only insofar as it helps the individuals who
compose it to achieve their personal destinies in this
world and in the next. A social theory which reduces the
function of society to a minimum of interference, to the
'hindering of hindrances', so as to allow complete freedom of action to the individual regardless of his duties
to society, does violence to the nature of man as a social
animal. But a social theory which reduces the individual
simply to a servant of the State, and defines his destiny
simply in terms of the good of the State, does violence
to the nature of man as a person, an immortal spirit whose
home is God. The second violence is the greater. So the
Church, while emphasizing man's duties to society, declares that 'in the last resort it is society which is for
man, and not man for society'. It affirms man's freedom,
not as a vague emotive slogan, but in the terms of clear-
cut rights with which the State may not interfere : the
right to a livelihood, the right to work (and to *creative*
work) of his own choosing, the right to freedom of
thought and conscience, the right to found and bring up
a family, the right of such ownership (as God's steward)
as will secure to him a dignified, free and stable future
for himself and his family. These freedoms the Church
upholds because man is *perfectissimum in natura*; and
because no created thing may cast into bondage those
whom God has made his sons.

But within the greatness of the human person, within

the 'unique self-subsistent', there is another paradox and
another tension. The greatness itself can be a misery. It
was said of Napoleon that he made one wonder whether
sovereigns could have a neighbour. The wages of greatness is loneliness. Of his nature man is outward-turning;
he can escape his destiny of becoming 'in a manner all
things' only at the cost of spiritual decay and death. Yet
he is enclosed in the loneliness of his uniqueness. At the
core of his nature there is the desire—an ontological longing—for oneness with other persons, with the race, with
the world, with God; at the same time he must equally
assert and cling to his identity. So, again, he is ceaselessly
torn in two opposite directions. For this is not the same
tension as that presented by the fact that man is both
social animal and individual person. A man can play his
part in society (though as we shall see he ought not)
without involving his whole self; he can be at surface-
level a citizen, and reserve to himself the deeper realities.
But this second tension exists within those deeper realities themselves: it is in his inmost being that he is
torn between the rival claims of the Self and the Other.
He can attempt to deny the claims of his selfhood; and
then he becomes, in personal relationships simply the
shadow and echo of another personality, in society the
sub-rational creature of the state- or race-deity; in religion he follows the path of the pantheist; in each case
he ceases to be a human being. Or he can deny the claims
of the Other; and so he becomes not a man but a mega-
phone, proclaiming his own greatness in a ghost-ridden
world. The danger of a tension is always that we may be
tempted not to resolve but to suppress it by suppressing
one of its terms; and these two extremes are the rival
dangers which have beset a humanity trying to escape its
paradox. If the east has tended in some degree to suppress the individual personality in its desire to find re-
integration in the Whole, the west has certainly tended
to ignore the Whole in its aggrandisement of the individual. That upsurge of worship of the self which begins

in the culture of the Renaissance, the philosophy of Descartes, the politics of Locke, the economics of *laissez-faire*, ends by degrading what it set out to exalt. Egocentricity, individualism, do not fulfil but empty the personality.

Yet *is* there a real solution to the paradox? Can a man, in those levels in which he is most unique, break through the bonds of his loneliness? The answer is not no; but neither is it an unqualified yes.

'To man the world is twofold, in accordance with his twofold attitude. The attitude of man is twofold, in accordance with the twofold nature of the primary words which he speaks . . . The one primary word is the combination *I-Thou*. The other primary word is the combination *I-It*; wherein, without a change in the primary word, one of the words *He* and *She* can replace *It* . . . Primary words do not signify things, but they intimate relations.' The world of *I-It* is the world of subject-object relations, the world of experience. But 'the man who experiences has no part in the world. For it is "in him" and not between him and the world that the experience arises.' If I consider a tree I can look on it as a picture, as movement, as an expression of law, or I can study it and classify it as a species; and in all this it remains my object. But it may come about, 'if I have both will and grace, that in considering the tree I become bound up in relation to it. The tree is no longer *It*.' So too 'if I face a human being as my *Thou*, and say the primary word *I-Thou* to him, he is not a thing among things . . . nor is he a nature able to be experienced and described, a loose bundle of named qualities. But with no neighbour, and whole in himself, he is *Thou* and fills the heavens. This does not mean that nothing exists except himself. But all else lives in *his* light . . . And just as prayer is not in time but time in prayer, sacrifice not in space but space in sacrifice, and to reverse the relation is to abolish the reality, so with the man to whom I say *Thou*. I do not meet with him at some time and place or other . . . I do not experience the man to whom I say *Thou*. But I take my stand in

relation to him, in the sanctity of the primary word . . .
All real living is meeting.'[1] Very wisely (unless we are
degrading words by abusing them) we say not that love
is in us but that we are in love.

Western man is so circumscribed, both by individual
training and by racial tradition, within the confines of
the world of subject-object relations that he finds the
word *I-Thou* obscure or meaningless. Yet it is the primitive word. We should find it easier could we remember
our first days and years of life. The Jews have a saying,
'In the mother's body man knows the universe, in birth
he forgets it.'[2] It is the 'shades of the prison-house' that
shut us off from the world of *I-Thou* and surround us
with a world of objects which cannot alleviate the loneliness of confinement within the Ego. We *may* indeed
escape the prison, or escape from the prison, in our wak-
ing as we do in our sleeping hours; but there is a force
which always presses us back towards the gates, a force
far more primitive than our modern western heritage
of thought which, indeed, without it could not have
come to be. It is the force of original sin. For it was sin
that broke up the harmony of creation into numberless
discordant fragments; it is sin that causes the self to proclaim itself supreme and autonomous, to assume sover-
eignty over the world it cannot govern; it is sin that robs
man of the clarity and humility and humour which would
have enabled him to remain also a child.

Those who speak of the Fall as a 'Fall upwards' are
emphasizing a truth of great value. It was indeed (being
pride—*super-bia*) a fall upwards in the sense that it was
a determination to scale the heights of conscious autonomy, to be independent of God and so to be absolute
arbiter of destiny. The goddess of reason is an entirely
immanent deity. She is also a bore, being quite unable to
laugh at herself. Absolute Man is a chimera posing as a

---

[1] M. Buber: *I and Thou*, pp. 3–11.
[2] cf. Buber, *op. cit.*, p. 25.

god (and therefore an amusing species of *ens rationis*), but incapable of appreciating the humour of the situation (and therefore tiresome). But the Fall was a fall upwards because it was the destruction of the child, not because it was the creation of the man. The complete man is *not* born out of the death of the child as ashes are made out of the destruction of wood. The complete man is born only through the continued existence of the child; for it is the child in him that makes him wise (and not merely well-informed) by keeping him humble, makes him creative by safeguarding his power to see and to receive, makes him (psychologically speaking) *capax Dei* by keeping him in mind of his nothingness. It is the child-man alone who is the human person: growing always in maturity, freedom, responsibility, but also growing always more childlike, more receptive, more completely one with the family of men, with the universe, with God. That is why the answer to the question, Can a man break through the bonds of his loneliness? is a qualified yes. He can do so; but, safely and fully, only through the redemptive grace of Christ. He will want to achieve the plenitude of his selfhood apart from God and in defiance of his essential dependence on God; he will want to use all other things and persons as means to this end; or at best he will want to love nature apart from man, or man and nature apart from God; and if he does so he will in fact be forcing himself further and further away from integrity. But through the grace of God he may be able to obey the command to 'become again as little children'; he may be able to 'lose his life', his egocentric, his would-be autonomous life, and so find his true life in the universe of Being. The Christian revelation solves the dilemma between the desire for God and the desire for personal integrity by revealing to us the meaning of the beatific vision. So too the dilemma of man who is part of the universe and yet not part of the universe, who is part of the human family and yet is unique and independent, who is infinitesimal and yet infinite, can be fully

solved only in the crucible of charity. 'Let charity make
thee a slave, since the Truth hath made thee free.' As
saints become saints through scrubbing floors, so man becomes infinite by lovingly choosing the infinitesimal. He
is both part and whole, but he can only be perfectly each
by being the other: he can only be perfectly a citizen
by being perfectly a person, independent in mind, mature in judgement, creative, responsible; he can only be
perfectly a person by being a citizen—and the child of a
family, of a race, of the universe, of the Church, of God:
for it is through living *in* these relations, through being
in love with these wholes, that he can himself be made
whole.

The Renaissance and the subsequent history of the west
stand for the aggrandisement of the individual. But the
aggrandisement of the individual is far from being the
same as—is indeed the precise contrary of—acknowledgement of the grandeur of the human person. A society has
a right to be called civilized when its members are real
personalities, really independent, responsible, creative
individuals, themselves making the life of society instead
of merely receiving their life from society. But in this
respect our society today seems to be not progressing but
regressing: the more the claims of the individual are ex-
tolled the more real personality seems to be at a discount: we are regimented in our work, standardized in
our clothes, passive recipients of standardized amusements and (unless we react violently and in time) uncritical consumers of the mawkish or commercial vulgar
ties of a standardized press. The person is ontologically
independent, self-subsistent; the whole purpose of society in general as of education in particular is to enable
him to become intellectually and morally independent
and self-subsistent too.

But the way to remedy the present standardization of
life is to become not more individualist but less. Individualism is the root of the disease: the remedy is per-
sonalism. The personality becomes deeper, richer, more

independent, not in so far as it tears itself from its roots
in the race, the universe, God, but on the contrary in so
far as it more and more recognizes and acknowledges
them and grows from them.

Quod enim (*homo*) *est*, says Boethius, *aliis debet quae
non sunt homo* : what man is he owes to other things
which are not man. The term self-subsistence in the definition of person often appears in Latin as *incommunica-
bilitas*; and though it would be a crass misunderstanding
to interpret this as an 'inability to communicate with
others'—it is a perfection, not a privation—it is none the
less useful to set it over against the 'communion of
saints', the *bonum commune*, the *unio* of lovers and of
the soul with God, as a reminder that when we have described the essential denotations of *personalitas* we are
far from having exhausted the connotations of personality. Self-subsistence is not self-sufficiency. What man is
he owes to other things which are not man, not *natura
humana*. We become, if we have will and power to do
so, what comes to us from without. 'All real living is meeting.' 'I become through my relation to the *Thou*.' The
personality becomes complete only in so far as it affirms
and enlarges the self in and by the very act of breaking
down the bonds of selfhood. It becomes complete only
by achieving oneness with nature and men and God and
then giving forth again of its fullness. It is then that it can
serve society, not with the officialdom of the bureaucrat,
with the power of personality of the saint. For sin will
always drag us back to our egocentricity until we live
fully in the charity of Him 'of whose fullness we have all
received'.

It is then no pious platitude to say that if we wish to
build a better world we must start from charity. Charity
does not mean kindly emotion; it does not primarily mean
kindly action towards others; it means a complete re-
orientation of attitude. We have seen the effects of individualism in practice; we have seen the effects of totali-
tarianism in practice; if we want neither of these, but a

world of real *persons*, then we first of all must turn our backs on the assumptions upon which these ways of life are built. Real democracy, if by democracy we mean a social system wherein every citizen shares in the task of creating and guiding the commonwealth, can only be achieved if all are free, responsible and creative servants of society, not simply as individuals exercising certain external functions, but as persons each of whom offers the uniqueness of his personality, as a *whole*, to the greater totality, the common work and the common weal, having achieved (yet still continuing to achieve more and more *through* his personal service) wholeness in himself through his ability to say the primary word *I-Thou* to his fellow men, to the world, to God.

12. ECCLESIASTICAL JARGON

Why do so many people leave the Church, not on account of some great crisis such as having to choose between it and a forbidden marriage, but simply by drifting away? To blame the prevailing climate of opinion in a post-Christian world is only to throw the question back further: why is there so little resistance to that climate? It seems likely that we must look for an answer in part at least to the way in which the faith was taught; for clearly the teaching cannot have bitten deep, cannot have evoked a deep response—not simply from the mind but from the whole personality—or it would not so easily be dislodged.

The Church teaches in two ways. It appeals to the reason with its creeds and formulas, its catechisms, its reasoned theology; it appeals to intuition with its symbols. Both appeals are essential, and it seems likely that the greatest flaw in our teaching lies in our neglect of the latter. How many Catholics really understand and live the Church's symbols or see their own lives in terms of that universal myth, that 'dark journey', which is brought to a divine fulfilment in the life, death and resurrection of our Lord and in the re-presenting and application of these, not merely *significative* but *effective*, to the souls of men in baptism and the sacrifice of the Mass? [1] But it seems likely also that there is a weakness in the method of our doctrinal teaching, and that the weakness lies in the kind of language we use to express that doctrine.

To put it bluntly, do we talk jargon? The answer seems undoubtedly to be yes. Jargon may be defined, first,

[1] cf. my *The Paradise Tree* for a full discussion of this point.

as technical language out of place.[2] Theologians need a technical language just as much as physicists, lawyers or logicians; but terms which are perfectly in place in the theological schools or textbooks may be quite out of place in the pulpit. A sermon may well be indigestible if it is packed tight with ponderous Latinisms—transubstantiation, redemption, salvation, damnation, absolution and so on—or with any difficult technical terminology. Sometimes it seems as though we go out of our way to make the realities we speak of as unreal as possible. There are examples in the list of the sacraments. *Confirmare* means to strengthen, but 'to confirm', nowadays, does not: it merely means to endorse, as you confirm a verbal order by a written one. *Poenitentia* is the sacrament not of penance but of repentance or, quite simply, of sorrow and forgiveness. Why must we say 'matrimony', as though it had nothing to do with marriage? Above all, why must we say 'extreme unction' when we know perfectly well that 'extreme' seldom suggests something coming at the end —one does not say at breakfast 'I am having my extreme piece of toast'—and that 'unction' suggests the oleaginous and evokes an image of Uriah Heep? Would it not be better to talk at least sometimes of the sacraments of strengthening, sorrow, marriage and last anointing?

Sometimes we use terms which are definitely misleading or which falsify the reality they are used to describe. A case in point is the second mystery of the rosary, which we call the visitation. A visitation normally means nowadays a divine punishment in the form of some catastrophe such as famine, flood or plague; or, in a narrower context, the descent upon a parish or religious community of high ecclesiastical authority for purposes of inspection. But quite apart from that, the ponderous word obscures the point of the story, which is its *homeliness* and the humility

[2] The next few pages are adapted from an article on 'Ecclesiastical Jargon' published in the *Clergy Review*, April 1957, with kind permission of the Editor.

of our Lady: immediately after the immensities of the first mystery she goes off with haste to help her cousin with the housework and with the preparations for the coming of the baby.[3]

Sometimes we forget that words change their meaning in the course of centuries. If we tell a boy nowadays to be meek and mild he will be likely to think that Christianity is a very sissy religion. If *devotio* is defined in terms of the will, devotion is hardly a proper translation since it has come to refer rather to the emotions. Purity, as the name of a virtue, has lost its original meaning of integrity, single-mindedness, something unalloyed, and come to mean simply sexual continence. Temperance will no longer do for *temperantia*, nor benevolence for *benevolentia*; and charity to most modern ears has lost all but a tiny fraction of the glory of *caritas*.

On an old, well-worn penny the image of king or queen may be quite obliterated; in the same way words and phrases can become *clichés* which in the end fail to evoke any real response at all and become on the contrary soporifics. To this class of jargon belong what might be called the pulpit bromides; certain pious ways of referring to God and holy things which are good enough in themselves but which have become automatic and therefore unalterable. If God, our Lord, our Lady, the Church, the Mass, the Pope are *always* referred to as Almighty God, our divine Redeemer, our blessed Lady, our holy Mother

[3] In reciting the rosary we could best avoid the long Latin words and at the same time make the titles of the decades more telling if we put them in the form of statements as we do in the Stations of the Cross. Thus: The Angel comes to Mary; Mary visits her cousin Elizabeth; Jesus is born; Jesus is taken to the Temple; Jesus is found in the Temple; Jesus endures his Agony in the Garden; Jesus is scourged (or flogged? cf. *infra*); Jesus is crowned with thorns; Jesus carries his cross; Jesus is crucified; Jesus rises again; Jesus goes to heaven; The Holy Ghost comes down upon the Apostles; our Lady is taken to heaven; our Lady is crowned Queen of Heaven.

the Church, the holy sacrifice of the Mass, our holy Father the Pope, these expressions come in the end to have this soporific effect. Marriage, in this sort of language, is always the sacrament of holy matrimony; sexual self-control is holy purity or, even worse, the holy virtue—which incidentally throws an interesting light on what is evidently an accepted scale of values, in practice if not in theory, where virtues and vices are concerned: all the supernatural virtues can be called holy, but if any one is to be singled out in this way over all the others it ought surely to be *caritas*? (One has even seen purity—in the modern Catholic sense, referred to as the angelic virtue, which is odd indeed, for if there is one virtue we *cannot* ascribe to spirits it is sexual continence.)

We suffer greatly—and why without protest it is difficult to see—from mistranslations.[4] Pictures are labelled *The Descent from the Cross*, presumably a mistranslation of *descente*; one even seems to recall seeing somewhere the ultimate infelicity of *The Invention of the True Cross*. It is not always necessary or even correct to translate an Italian or Italo-Latin superlative by an English most; yet this is almost invariably done, sometimes with disastrous results as in the phrase 'her most chaste spouse' which implies that there were other spouses of rather lower grade. In the same way 'Blessed be his most sacred heart' really implies a polycardiac condition. In the end, 'most' itself becomes a bromide, not enhancing but on the contrary blanketing the meaning of the adjective it accom-

---

[4] A correspondent has sent in this gem from an official translation of the *Ingraviscentibus Malis* of Pope Pius XI : 'Very admirable is this crown interwoven with the angelic salutation which is interposed in the Sunday prayer': even the well-instructed catholic, who will doubtless quickly identify the angelic salutation with the *Hail Mary*, may not so quickly realize that 'the Sunday prayer' is in fact the *Our Father*, the translator having presumably got into a slight muddle over the adjective 'dominical'; what 'interposed in' could conceivably mean must, as the correspondent remarks, 'always remain a mystery'.

panies. In what is called 'bop' language, 'most' also looms large and has been elevated to the dignity of a noun; if one wants to ascribe excellence to a jazz drummer or trumpeter one says of him, 'Man, that cat's the real most', which, if somewhat bizarre, has a certain freshness about it; in ecclesiastical jargon the word is dead; it falls, like a pebble into a pool, with a little plop. It infests the litany of Loreto, which in any case is marred by mistranslations and ugliness which reach their nadir with 'Singular vessel of devotion'. 'Mother inviolate' inevitably suggests to the ear a violet dress, just as the reference in another prayer to our spiritual forebears as delivering to us inviolate the faith of the Holy Roman Church' suggests a sort of perpetual Lent. 'Amiable', with its slightly pejorative overtones ('an amiable lunatic'), will not do for *amabilis*; nor is 'admirable' the same as *admirabilis*. (Needless to say, we have in fact 'most amiable' and 'most admirable'.) 'Most venerable' nowadays suggests a long white beard, and will not do for *veneranda*.[5]

[5] In an article in *Worship* (U.S.A.) on the current English version of the litany of Loreto and its need of revision I ventured to put forward the following tentative suggestions for the invocations which seem for various reasons ill translated:

Sancta Virgo virginum	Holiest of all virgins
Mater divinae gratiae	Mother of God's Grace
Mater purissima	Mother of perfect love
Mater castissima	Mother of flawless chastity
Mater inviolata	Mother ever a Maiden
Mater intemerata	Mother unsullied by evil
Mater amabilis	Mother so loveable
Mater admirabilis	Mother so wonderful
Virgo prudentissima	Virgin most wise
Virgo veneranda	Virgin whom we revere
Virgo praedicanda	Virgin whose praises we sing
Virgo potens	Virgin so powerful
Virgo clemens	Virgin so gentle
Virgo fidelis	Virgin so true
Speculum iustitiae	Mirror of holiness
Sedes sapientiae	Fountain of wisdom
Causa nostrae laetitiae	Source of our Joy

Our 'devotions'—why should they not be called prayers?—abound in examples of the kind of language which bears no relation to everyday speech and which therefore creates a sense of unreality. In the prayers for England read on the second Sunday of the month we hear the priest praying that our Lady's name may be 'lisped by little ones'. Apart from the unfortunate winsomeness to modern ears of 'littles ones', this request proves on inspection to be a very strange one. First of all, it is true that some children lisp, but many do not, so why should this affliction be ascribed to them all? But on a closer inspection one finds that the prayer is not just saying that they do lisp but praying that they *shall* lisp, which is wrong, for we are not allowed to pray that disaster may befall our neighbour. But even this is not all, for if we look yet again at the phrase we realize we are praying for an absolute impossibility: no one, child or adult, can possibly lisp the word 'Mary'.

Again, our most popular hymns abound in examples of bad language and false sentiment. When for instance we pray that 'earthly joys may fade away' do we mean what we are saying? Parents spend all their time and money trying to make their children happy, and lovers do the same for each other, and then they come to church and find themselves praying that all their efforts may be frustrated. Again it is one thing to declare our determination to be true till death to the faith of the English martyrs; it is quite another to say, How sweet would be their children's fate (we ourselves, presumably, being the children in question) if they like them could die for it. Have we in fact such heroic fortitude? And one is left speech-

Vas spirituale	Chalice of spiritual life
Vas honorabile	Chalice of honour
Vas insigne devotionis	Splendid chalice of dedication
Regina sine labe originali concepta	Queen in whom was never stain of sin
Regina in caelos assumpta	Queen taken up into heaven

less at the thought of what image of celestial surgery could have invaded the mind of the writer of a hymn to the Heart of Mary when he (or she) penned the line,

Within thy Heart enclose my own, to keep it
chaste and pure.

But perhaps by now we should be inured to the lyrical flights of what might be called the surgical school of devotional writers : a form of prayers which has long been in use for making the Stations of the Cross, begs Christ to nail our hearts to his feet; and indeed it is noticeable how, with writers of this school, the slightest mention of the heart seems to go, like strong wine, straight to the head.

The plain—indeed downright ugly—fact is that sentimentality must have so far run away with us that often we just do not think what we are saying, for if we did we should realize that what we are saying is often either nonsense or else a lie. That dreadful expression 'The Prisoner of the Tabernacle' again implies something quite false : for though a man may, because of his convictions, choose to go to prison he will not go without reluctance unless he is a pathological case; and in any case the implication that reservation is in some way a confining of God, and his emergence from the Tabernacle a liberation, is just monstrous.

It would be a tragic error to regard all this as just of aesthetic or pedantic interest. It is of the deepest and most urgent importance to the Church; for if the doctrinal and devotional language we use is such as to make our religion seem utterly unreal we cannot be surprised that people should abandon it. It is essential then, in preaching, teaching and worship, to try to put eternal truths, traditional doctrines, perennial aspirations, into contemporary, down-to-earth English. In his introduction to the *Letters to Young Churches* of Mr. J. B. Phillips (itself an outstanding example of how the thing *can* be done) Mr. C. S. Lewis writes, *à propos* of the Authorized Version :

'Beauty exalts, but beauty also lulls. Early associations endear but they also confuse. Through that beautiful solemnity the transporting or horrifying realities of which the Book tells may come to us blunted and disarmed and we may only sigh with tranquil veneration when we ought to be burning with shame or struck dumb with terror or carried out of ourselves by ravishing hopes and adorations. Does the word "scourged" really come home to us like "flogged"? Does "mocked him" sting like "jeered at him"?' With us Catholics, alas, the problem is that of being lulled not so much by beauty as by a familiar ugliness, not so much by solemnity of language as by a jargon which is remote from reality and sometimes meaningless.

One sometimes hears it said, not by disaffected but by good, though sad and troubled, Catholics that they feel their priests live in a world and talk in a language quite remote from the cares, problems, ways of thought, of the everyday world of the layman. If this is so it means that an abyss separates clergy from laity, an abyss which can only grow wider and deeper as time goes on unless we take drastic measures.

What is it that makes us cling so stubbornly and relentlessly to the stock phrase of the theological textbooks, the cumbrous Latinisms of catechetical and pulpit bromides, the false sentimental *clichés* and linguistic barbarisms of our hymns and 'devotions'? Sometimes perhaps it is mental laziness : it is so much easier to let sleeping *clichés* lie, in both senses, than to embark on the painful process of creating something new and true. But sometimes perhaps it is a misplaced sense of reverence, a feeling that it would be impious to change long-established forms of words; and perhaps this feeling is in part due to a confusion of thought concerning the mutability or immutability of quite different *kinds* of formulas. The sacramental formulas, the actual Latin words used in the moment of baptizing, of absolving from sin, of consecrating bread and wine, are obviously in a class of their own and need not be considered here; but what of forms of prayer in our own language? If we spoke our Lord's native Aramaic and were certain of the exact words in which he gave us the *Our Father* (the versions in *Matthew* and *Luke* are in fact different) we should be hesitant indeed to make any change in them; but this does not apply to translations: these could be regarded as (relatively) immutable only because of very great antiquity (as for instance one can hardly imagine changes in the Latin *Canon* of the Mass) or of very great beauty. Even then we might need, and almost certainly should need, a new version from time to time to jog us out of that numbing of the senses which the over-familiar so easily induces in us; and the point to be stressed is surely that the making of a new version, far from implying disrespect with regard to the old, may on the contrary be our best way of showing reverence towards the old. The best way of showing love and reverence for our Lord's own prayer is to make sure that the *sense* of what he said really strikes home.

This is especially relevant to the educating of children in the faith. Few adults would wish to change, for their own use, the form of the *Our Father* to which we are all accustomed; but we ought to ask ourselves and with some urgency—whether for children it might not be better to start off with a simpler version, using only the sort of words they normally use in everyday life; and the same question applies *a fortiori* to other prayers, to the creed, and as far as possible to the catechism. How meaningful to a young child can it be to say 'hallowed be thy name', 'our trespasses', 'the fruit of thy womb', 'through my most grievous fault', 'who was conceived of the holy Ghost'? Yet the essential meaning of such phrases *can* be conveyed in simple terms—and if it were we may surmise that it would not only be children who would benefit. Would it not be wise to teach small children, and even sometimes to use ourselves in our private prayer, some such rendering of (for example) *Our Father, Hail Mary, Glory be, Credo* and *Confiteor* as the following:

Our Father in heaven,
we pray that everyone may praise you,
            and obey you as their king,
            and do whatever you say,
on earth as they do in heaven.
Give us today the food we need,
and forgive us for what we have done wrong,
   as we forgive the people who have done wrong to us;
and keep us safe from sin and from all that is bad.

Holy Mary, you are very close and dear to God;
you are blessed, more than all other women,
and blessed in Jesus, your Son.
Holy Mother of God, pray for us now
   and when the time comes for us to die,
that even though we are sinners we may go to heaven.

We praise and honour God our Father,
            and Jesus our Lord,
            and the holy Spirit of Love,
now and always.

I believe in God who is our Father and who made
   heaven and earth.
I believe in his Son, Jesus Christ, our Lord,
   who through the power of the holy Spirit
   came into our world, and our Lady was his mother.
I believe that he was crucified and died and was buried;
   but that the third day after he died he rose again,
   and that then he went up into heaven,
   and that he reigns there now as our king with his Father,
   but that he will come again one day to judge all men.
I believe in the holy Spirit,
      in the catholic Church,
      in the saints' love for us all;
I believe that God will forgive us our sins if we
   are sorry for them, and will take us one day, body
   and soul, to live with him for ever in heaven.

Dear Lord, I want to tell you,
        and our Lady,
        and the great St. Michael the angel,
        and St. John Baptist,
        and the apostles SS. Peter and Paul
        and all the other saints,
that I have sinned
  in things I've thought
  and things I've said
  and things I've done.
And so I ask our Lady, and St. Michael, St. John,
  SS. Peter and Paul and all the other saints
  to pray for me to you, our Lord and God.

As in prayer so also in the teaching of doctrine we can try to get away from ponderous Latinisms and to express their meaning in simple English, so that our words may act not like a soporific lulling our hearers to sleep but as a goad spurring them to think for themselves, to assimilate and to absorb. Certainly it is only if we do manage to dig deep below the surface, if our hearers do manage to assimilate and absorb the deep realities of which we try to speak, that there is much hope of their retaining what they hear and living it.

Why then, once again, do we cling to our stock phrases and our *clichés*? There is mental laziness, there is the misplaced sense of reverence : is there perhaps also fear to be reckoned with, fear of being accused of heterodoxy ? If we stick rigidly to the accepted Latinisms—hypostatic union, sanctifying grace, actual graces, perfect contrition, beatific vision, penitential exercises, ejaculatory prayers —we can feel secure, we can be sure that at least we are not teaching heresy. Yes, but we pay a heavy price for our security if in fact we teach nothing at all : if our instructions leave the children bewildered and uncomprehending, the adults bored either to sleep or to tears. We pay a heavy price if from dozing through sermons, instructions, devotions, the people end by drifting away

altogether. And is it not a fact that that does happen?
That is why the problem is so urgent: the eternal estate
of many souls may depend on whether we do something
about it, and how quickly and with what success.

13. ON TEACHING THROUGH PARABLES

'All these things Jesus spoke in parables to the multitudes : and without parables he did not speak to them.'[1] In the days when Lagrange was writing his commentaries on the gospels he was obliged, in treating of our Lord's parables, to argue against the view, held by such writers as Buzy, that Christ used this mode of preaching in order to *hide* the truth from his hearers, to *punish* them. Nowadays we are no longer puzzled, though we must still be distressed, by the words of Isaiah, that 'hearing they may hear, and not understand' : we see them for what they are, the expression of a sad divine irony. But what may well puzzle us about this theory that the parables were in effect designed to obfuscate is that apparently it never struck the exponents of it as strange that the Church should have gone through the ages 'punishing' and 'obfuscating' the faithful by continuing to use the parables year by year in so many of its Sunday gospel-readings.

Lagrange for his part wrote of the 'gentle considerateness', *le mode si miséricordieux*, of this form of preaching, 'so well adapted to simple, uncultured people' and seeming obscure to many of Christ's hearers only because 'their hearts did not come to the help of their minds';[2] and these remarks suggest a question about our own preaching methods today : if our Lord thought it best to preach in this way to the multitudes, and the Church in its gospel-readings continues to do so, should not preachers today generally speaking follow suit ? (For it is likely that the majority of those they address will be,

[1] *Matt.* xiii, 34 (Douai).
[2] Lagrange : *The Gospel of Jesus Christ*, p. 171.

if not unlettered, at any rate not highly cultured.) This is not to suggest that every preacher should attempt to convey doctrinal truth to the people in parables of his own devizing (heaven forbid!): parable is one of the many forms of 'picture-language', of what can roughly be called the poetic as against the prose use of words: the question then is whether the preacher, though not himself a maker of parable or poetry, should not at least concern himself with parables *as poetry* instead of restricting himself to reasoned expositions of such doctrinal or moral points as may be suggested by them. Those who failed to appreciate our Lord's parables did so because their *hearts* were at fault: the essential point about this mode of preaching is precisely that it does appeal to the heart as well as to the mind: intuition and (at a deep level) feeling are engaged as well as reason. (It is necessary thus to qualify 'feeling' lest it be taken as meaning a superficial or cheap or perhaps quite false sentimentality: we are all familiar on the one hand with the kind of sermon which is in fact and perhaps also in name an instruction, appealing simply to the mind, and on the other hand with the *ferverino* which may evoke simply a superficial and transient emotion without any lasting effect at all; the parables, like all great poetry, art, music, appeal to the whole personality and, from those who have eyes to see and ears to hear, evoke a total response.)

The *ferverino* may doubtless be of great value in certain circumstances for bringing about a needed 'change of heart'; but its value must depend on the degree to which its emotional appeal impels the hearer to go on to something deeper, to a true *metanoia*, a true change of mind and will.

As for instruction, reasoned expositions of dogma and morals, their necessity is obvious; some of the dangers which confront the preacher today in giving them were discussed in the last chapter; the relevant point we must consider now, is that even when they are well done, when the preacher has the wave-length of his audience and they feel that he is dealing with vital issues in a vital way and respond accordingly, still the enlightenment he has given them may go no further than their minds and have no effect on their wills and therefore their conduct.

A leader-writer in *The Tablet* of March 28th, 1959, commenting on an article in *The Month* by the late Ronald Knox, remarked that 'imagination is a dangerous word: this is easily thought to mean no more than fanciful, unreal and arbitrary constructions', whereas in reality it is 'a faculty through which truth can be discerned and appreciated, more potent for religious truth than the discursive reason on which so much exclusive reliance has been placed'; the 'concern of pastors and masters', he continued, must be to ensure that those they teach will 'think of their religion in all its breadth and depth, not as an intellectual explanation which they will come to drop as no explanation, but as what it professes to be: a guide to right living, a faith by which to live with the heart and will as well as with the mind.'

Msgr. Knox himself was disquieted at the Catholic habit of talking of 'instruction'—it is significant that the school periods set aside for the discussion of religious matters are in some schools known as RI, seeming to imply that there is in fact no real discussion at all and that what the pupils are given is something severely and exclusively intellectual—and, quoting the words 'Did not our hearts burn within us when he talked with us by the way?', he wrote of what he thought the Catholic 'apologist' ought to be like: 'He will vindicate the prophecies, not by raking up a score of familiar quotations, but by exhibiting the Old Testament *in extenso* as a cipher message imposed on history. He will prove the divineness of our Lord's mission, not by presenting us with a series of logical dilemmas, but by trying to reconstruct the picture of our Lord himself; what it was that met the gaze of the apostles, and the touch of their hands. He will read the New Testament, not as a set of "passages" which must somehow be reconciled with one another, but as the breathless confidences of living men, reacting to human situations, and inflamed with zeal for their Master. He will portray the teaching Church, not as a harassed official "handing out" information at a series of press conferences, but as a patient pioneer washing out the gold from the turbid stream of her own memories. Everything will come alive at his touch; he will not merely know what he is talking about, but feel what he is talking about.'

The parables, and Christ's teaching in general, go direct to the deeper levels (unless the hearer is wilfully deaf or atrophied with regard to them) because they make use not merely of concepts but of 'poetic' images, symbols, which do lie deep indeed in us all whether we are conscious of the fact or not. If then, like the seed falling on good ground, they find a receptive ear, the response they evoke will be neither merely intellectual nor merely emotional but personal, involving the whole personality.

Now the mention of symbols or picture-language sometimes provokes an unfavourable reaction because of an ambiguity about the terms: picture-language may be taken to mean flowery language, sentimental or rhetorical trimmings, and the reaction may then (justifiably) be: Why can't we have the pure word, and cut out the frills? In fact, a clear distinction has to be made between two quite different types of symbol, which might perhaps be roughly described as innate, natural (in the sense of following the pattern of reality-as-we-know-it) on the one hand, and invented or arbitrary on the other. Some of the Fathers, for instance, allegorized the parables: they did not merely elucidate what was already there, explaining the allegorical elements which many of the parables in fact contain; they added to what was there, inventing an allegorical meaning for this or that detail so as to draw some suitable moral lesson from it in their sermons. Again, the very expression 'flowery language' reminds us of the 'language of flowers' (whether sacred or profane), and this also, apart from one or two examples, is arbitrary enough. Even in the parables themselves some of the detail, familiar ground to the original audience, may seem strange to many today. But to think of the great universal symbols as embellishments of—and therefore possibly distractions from—the naked word of truth is to misunderstand their nature completely. When our Lord speaks of water we cannot but be reminded of the reality of baptismal rebirth; when he says wood or tree we hear redemption; wine is inescapably for us the sacred banquet, the marriage feast.

Yet when he speaks of these things he speaks in mystery: not only in the sense that these things which once were elements in the pagan mysteries are now embodied and shine forth in the radiance of the Christian Mystery, but also in the more colloquial sense that they are not clear-cut, neat and tidy, immediately apprehensible; we stand before them like Nicodemus, questioning, until, having looked long and listened long, we are able to enter into them. For these symbols are of their nature ambivalent: the water is both the terrible, destructive tempest and the gentle sea pacific, both the devouring flood and the refreshing spring; the fire is the splendour of Phoebus the life-bringer but also the torture of the scorching, shrivelling flames; wine can rejoice the heart or destroy the reason; the wood is both death and life. Creation is described for us (and the description applies also to re-creation) in terms of cutting, cleaving (*bara*): the knife produces life, the tomb is the womb; our Lord spoke to the multitudes in paradox, because for us, who see only as in a glass, reality *is* paradoxical: complex, untidy, full of problems and tangles to which there is no complete solution in this world. And this applies even—perhaps one should say this applies above all—to our apprehension, such as it is, of the divine reality: when we say for instance that in God justice and mercy are one we state what we know must be true, but we cannot see *how* it is true, though at the same time we know we shall not be in the truth if we think of God simply as justice, forgetting mercy, or as mercy in despite of justice. Christ is both Judge and Good Shepherd; both divine Door and the One who himself knocks at our human doors; if we cannot make a single picture out of these apparently contradictory aspects at least we must keep both aspects simultaneously in our minds and hearts.

Is not this another substantial advantage which the parabolic sermon has over the other two types, perhaps especially in these days when men are made so aware—often so agonizingly aware—of the complexity of our existence, the *chiaroscuro* in which all of us, even those in whom faith and hope and love are at their strongest, must live? Too easily the reasoned exposition of a dogmatic truth or a moral principle can seem glib or at least too smooth and neat, too remote from the tangles and muddles of real life, to be true. Certainly, if one were giving a reasoned exposition of the idea of God's justice one could and doubtless should go on to speak of God's mercy; but one might run the risk then of leaving the hearer with the feeling that 'it was all very mysterious and contradictory', which means in effect that he would conclude it was all beyond him and would think no more about it; in any case it might well lack the impact of direct confrontation with the divine paradox, the ruthlessness of 'till thou repay the last farthing' together with the compassionate tenderness of the 'joy in heaven upon one sinner that doth penance, more than upon ninety-nine just who need not penance'.

Was not the brother of the prodigal son justified when he grumbled at his father's prodigality to the returned wastrel and at the inequity of his own case? At one ethical level, yes, of course. Was not Judas right when he spoke of the 'waste' of the ointment and of the needs of the poor? At one ethical level, again yes. Is it fair that the repentant sinner should be preferred to the ninety-nine just, that the harlots and sinners should be the first to enter the kingdom, that all the labourers should have received every man a penny, that the immediate possession of paradise should be promised not to those who had long and faithfully followed and served the Saviour but to a thief? At the divine level, yes. 'My thoughts are not your thoughts: nor your ways my ways, saith the Lord. For as the heavens are exalted above the earth, so are my ways exalted above your ways, and my thoughts above your thoughts. And as the rain and the snow come down from heaven, and return no more thither, but soak the earth, and water it, and make it to spring, and give seed to the sower, and bread to the eater: so shall my word be.'[3]

The purely human level, the level of the eye-for-an-eye, the level of justice-despoiled-of-mercy—these are not the divine level revealed to us in Christ. God is love; and love is itself paradox to us: is gentle and hard, healing and hurting, splendour and misery, exaltation and abasement; it is the bringer of joy and sorrow, of pain and ecstasy; it is light and darkness, *chiaroscuro*, for those who journey in *huius saeculi nocte*, in the night of this world; but *because* it is these contradictory things for us it is the rain and the snow, the water springing up, *saliens in vitam aeternam*, the seed for the sower, the bread for the eater; and that is why 'the mountains and hills shall sing praise' for us, as though each another Calvary, and 'all the trees of the country shall clap their hands' as sharing in the *mysterion tou staurou*, the mystery of the cross, as kin of the Tree of Life.

But to return: we cannot expect the preacher to be himself a parable-maker, a great poet: how then can we expect his preaching to be 'parabolic'? Because his is a humbler role, and in that humble role there are two things of great value (and, once again, of great value especially in these days) that he can do. First, his business is to be, in the original sense of the word, a pedagogue: the slave whose duty it was to lead the boy safely to his school. Our school is Christ, the Word and his words: the function of

[3] *Isaiah*, lv, 8–11 (Douai).

the preacher is to lead us to that Word, those words. The purpose of the homily, following immediately on the gospel-reading, as an integral part of the Mass is surely just that : to help the faithful to penetrate more deeply than before into the mystery which has just been shown forth to them; not (if for instance the reading has been a parable) to embroider it, but to help the hearers to be more capable of receiving it. A parable is a poem, and you cannot paraphrase a poem without destroying it, but you can be a pedagogue, you can point the way, just as a man who is not himself a painter but who loves and understands great paintings can help us towards discovering them in our turn.

Secondly, as we can be helped not only to appreciate this or that carving in stone but also to appreciate the stone itself out of which the carvings are made, so the preacher can concern himself not only with this or that parable or paradox but with the symbols which are the material of many parables and paradoxes; and this, one would argue, is certainly of urgent importance today for us who live in a world which psychologically is so warped and atrophied, still darkened by the shadows of postivism and empiricism, bedevilled by *scientisme*, conditioned to assume that scientific or rational processes of thought alone have any validity for 'real' life. It is painful to think of the abysmal contrast between the obviously immense impact of, say, the rite of baptism on the early Christian and the probable impact or lack of impact of the same rite on the Christian who is present at it today : for the early Christian the raw material of the rite, its symbolism, was already, if he were a Jew, as familiar as a native tongue, for through his study of the Bible he would have been steeped in it from childhood; if he were a convert from paganism he would still be likely to find it familiar enough from his knowledge of pagan mysteries or mythology; today, even if the difficulty of the use of Latin is overcome or circumvented, the rite may all too easily seem wholly strange, words and actions alike be in a

wholly unfamiliar idiom; for us, alone of all the races
and civilizations in human history, water, oil, fire, wind-
breath-spirit, may evoke no immediate vital response,
carry no immediate depth of meaning. What indeed
could seem more remote from these realities than our
world of technocracy and bureaucracy, of tinfoil and cel-
lophane, of popular press and pulp magazines, commer-
cials and subliminal advertizing, of reefers and teenage
gangs and the beat generation, of Hollywood and television situation-comedies, of sob-sisters and snob-sisters,
of beauticians and morticians, of the political bandwagon
and the economic rat-race and the *trahison des clercs*
and the death of culture?

But if Catholics, nurtured and educated in their faith
from childhood, find these realities remote from them we
cannot put all the blame on their environment: there
must surely be something lacking in that training itself.
Have not those of us who represent the 'teaching
Church', perhaps ourselves affected by the climate of
opinion and the standard of values into which we were
born, forgotten some essential element in our pedagogy?
And in particular, in our necessary concern for and ab-
sorption in such questions as the historicity of the Bible
have we perhaps forgotten precisely that the Bible is a
poem? Have we concentrated so exclusively on fact and
events as such as to neglect images, so that for us too the
images have become a 'forgotten language'? If so, we
must surely become pupils again before we can be adequate pedagogues: must 'discover' the Bible afresh, must
discover for instance that 'insignificant' historical details
in the Old Testament stories are not insignificant at all
because they are not merely historical. Forget for a moment the aspect of historicity and the problems it raises,
and concentrate on the images: and how the text leaps
into life, *saliens in vitam*, like the waters springing up into
life everlasting, like the 'roes and the harts of the fields',
like the hero of the *Song of Songs*, 'leaping upon the
mountains, skipping over the hills'!

Abraham rode to the hill of sacrifice, the 'mount of vision', on a donkey, as did the boy David to the camp of Saul, and as Christ into Jerusalem: riding on an animal constantly recurs in human imagery as a symbol of mastering and integrating our animal, our lower nature,[4] but this is a donkey, not a black horse, or a white charger: is all this insignificant? And Balaam's donkey rebuked him: what a waste if we spend our time and energy thrashing out the probability or improbability of this being an historical incident instead of diving deep into the image! When the promise was made to Abraham, Sara stood behind the door: and the 'door' is the *porta caeli*, gate of heaven, the hole made in the firmament that the rain may come down from heaven and make the earth to spring and give seed and bread to the eater: we have to go through the door, out into life, into the Presence, not hide away from it as we are so easily tempted to do, for if we hide behind it—burying our heads ostrich-like in the 'outward forms and modes of religion' or retreating behind this or that rationalization, prevarication, refusal—it becomes not a gate of heaven but a veil of the Temple which we will not allow to be rent for us.[5] Sara laughed at the promise, laughed it to scorn; as the boy Chanaan had laughed at Noah's nakedness, as the people laughed at 'the maid is not dead, but sleepeth', as the passers-by laughed at the Man on the cross; but the child, Isaac, was born and his name means Laughter, a Laughter which Abraham was called upon to surrender but which was restored to him. (How often do we preach

[4] cf. *supra*, chapter 1: the legend of Padre Patufet. The return, or desire to return, to the womb can be either a retreat *from* reality, corresponding to the death-wish or a search *for* reality, for life-through-death: Patufet or Jonah: Patufet's echoing (in an opposite sense) of the words of Isaiah quoted above is striking: we *have* to have the snow and the rain from heaven (we have to go out of doors and get uncomfortably wet) if we want to spring to life and be fruitful.

[5] cf. *ibid.*

about laughter, the two kinds, the black and the radiant, even though we have Dante's *luce eterna che ami ed arridi* to spur us on?)

Do we spend all our time arguing whether or in what way Jacob's lie to his father can be morally justified, or do we try to enter into the story-as-symbol? (Augustine's *non est mendacium, sed mysterium* could be taken as a glib debating reply or, on the contrary, as going straight to the heart of the matter; it is when we gaze at this episode as at a great painting, trying to apprehend it *in figura*, as a symbol, that we begin to grasp something of its immense typological and psychological and spiritual significance.) And Jacob saw in sleep a ladder (and the Lord 'leaning upon the ladder') and when he woke cried trembling, 'How terrible is this place! this is no other but the house of God, and the gate of heaven'; and he set up the stone, on which his head had rested, *in titulum*, as a monument, pouring oil upon the top of it; and then proceeding towards the east he saw a well in a field, and on the mouth thereof a great stone which later, prodigiously, he removed unaided: are we to see these details as insignificant, or rather as charged with an immensity of vital meaning?

If the latter then surely we should apply to all this the injunction to 'preach the word . . . in season, out of season'.[6] For if the preacher can communicate to his hearers his own awareness of and participation in the vital significance of the door, the well, the water, the stone, the oil, the wine, the laughter, and all the other great symbols which we meet again and again in the imagery of the Bible; and if he can help them to see, in this light, first the pattern of the Passion-story and then their own sharing in the daily life of the Church, the stone of their own churches and altars, the water of their own fonts, the oil of their sacramental strengthening, the bread and wine of their eucharistic offering and the di-

[6] II *Tim.* iv, 2 (Douai).

vine banquet which follows it, then surely the idiom of
Christian sacramentalism cannot remain for them a for-
eign tongue but must evoke from them its divinely intended response.

More than that, if the preacher goes on to convey
through these things some insight into the paradoxes of
Love, some glimpse of the ways of God with men, then
surely he can at least feel certain that his words will not
be written off as glib or unreal, remote from the tangled
problems, the fundamental untidiness, of life *in via*: he
will be truly a pedagogue in Christ's service, for he will
have led his hearers to Christ and therefore to some
awareness, in and through Christ, of the infinite immensity but also of the immediately impinging and invading
reality of the God who shakes the mountains but is also
the gentle brooding Dove, the *mysterium tremendum*
dwelling in light inaccessible who is also the baby in
swaddling clothes and the man on the tree, the burning
and consuming fire who is at the same time the warmth
and welcoming solace of the sea pacific, the terror and
majesty who also suffers and weeps with his creatures
and who in the end wipes away all tears from the eyes of
those who have sought him sorrowing, and gives himself
to them for ever to be their happiness and home.

14. THE SPIRIT-WORLD

Belief in the existence of spirits is nowadays at a discount : most people would consider the question if at all only in the very etiolated form of whether ghosts exist. Christians, committed by Bible and tradition alike to believing in angels bad and good, are sometimes uncomfortable about this doctrine and tend to give it little more than a notional assent while forgetting about it in practice. Where Satan is concerned this reluctance may be due to a basically false picturing of him either as the Evil Principle of the dualist religions or as the little red devil with horns and tail and pitchfork of medieval popular imagery rather than as the mighty but fallen created spirit, the brilliant, twisted intellect, with whom Christ wrestled in the wilderness.[1] Yet we may find even the true picture hard to accept inasmuch as the climate of opinion in which we live is opposed to the acceptance of anything that is not visible and tangible ; and we ought therefore to ask ourselves explicitly whether this contemporary disbelief is a happy example of modern enlightenment, a liberation of the mind from crude superstitions, or whether it is itself a crude refusal to face facts, a sort of 'It can't happen here' applied not to material but to spiritual occurrences. Primitive societies tend to attribute disease and death to the activity of ghost-souls or demons, to regard epilepsy, hysteria, madness as forms of diabolic possession. Modern western man, though he can be said to be emerging now from the darkness of nineteenth-century positivism and *scientisme*, still tends to think that all phenomena are either explicable by science

[1] cf. G. Vann and P. K. Meagher : *Stones or Bread ?*, chapter 1.

or else do not exist.[2] Which of the two views is the cruder?

Certainly if we set any store by the verdict of history we shall not lightly dismiss all belief in spirits as childishness. In the first place we have come belatedly to recognize that primitive societies are not necessarily 'benighted savages', that they may have a kind of knowledge and wisdom which our own society has long since lost, and that they sometimes regard our ways, our *mores*, with amused contempt. Secondly, we are the only historical civilization to have brushed aside belief in spirits as childish delusion; and we are only one among many such civilizations and not necessarily the most enlightened of them—indeed it is pitifully easy to make out a strong case for our being the least. (It is a healthily humbling exercise to reflect, for instance on the probable reactions of let us say Plato, Sophocles, Virgil, Augustine, Ausonius, Leonardo, Bach, Mozart, Rabelais, Voltaire—to say nothing of an Eckhart or a John of the Cross—if they were to find themselves thrust into one of our suburban shopping centres or grimier industrial cities at the rush-hour, or into one of our more popular seaside resorts in the summer—or, for that matter, made to listen to our radio programmes uninterruptedly for a fortnight. It is equally salutary to read what some of the more trenchant exponents of other contemporary civilizations have to say about our own.)

In ancient times the belief in spirits can be said to have been universal, and the worship of them common: Assyria had its 'secret' religion in which a whole hierarchy of evil spirits were worshipped; Chaldaea and Egypt are especially associated with magic; in Persia, Zoroastrianism (which still exists among the Parsees) laid emphasis on the dualist conflict between good and evil in the spirit-world; Rome had its magicians, as is shown by the stories and references in its literature and by imperial

2 cf. *supra*, chapter 3.

decrees against soothsayers; as for the Hebrews, while the concept of evil spirits as entities distinct both from God and from his good angels seems to emerge only gradually,[3] there is the mysterious reference to satyrs or 'hairy ones' in *Isaiah*, there is Saul's visit to the witch of Endor, and in apocryphal literature and tradition we meet Lilith, the spirit of night who was supposed to have been Adam's first wife (and who corresponds to the Babylonian night-demon Lilitu) and various legends of lamias, vampires and multitudinous spirits; these vampires also figure largely (together with werewolves, trolls and goblins) in Slav and Nordic legends.

Thus Christianity began its history in a world in which the existence of spirits, of supernatural powers, was taken for granted and which believed that men could invoke these powers and operate through them. Charles Williams, in his *Witchcraft*, divided such executants into four classes: first, 'the merely vile kind, the night-hags, the potion and poison makers'; secondly, 'the grander kind, such as the priestess in Virgil, learned in conjurations', able to 'control the heights and depths of things, change kingdoms, and even terrify the gods'; next, 'the diviners and astrologers, those who forecast the future and read the purposes of the stars'; fourthly, 'some few to whom the magical art was indeed "high-priestess of heaven", who, pushed on by a pure learning, followed in honour and chastity towards a sublime union with the final absolute power'.[4] To these different modes of commerce with another world must be added the 'tradition of a great and awful blasphemy—of the sexual union of alien and opposed natures':[5] that travesty of the doctrine of the Incarnation which figures so largely in the history of medieval witchcraft and satanism.

This is not the place to follow that history in detail nor

[3] cf. V. White: *God and the Unconscious*, chapter x.
[4] Williams *op. cit.*, p. 30.   [5] *ibid.*

to examine all the issues involved in it, the explicit or implicit pact with the devil, the familiars, the *maleficium* or working of harm through images, the sabbats, the night-riding, the worship of Satan, though to some of these we shall return later on. The point to be stressed for the moment is that Christianity was in no doubt as to the reality of supernatural powers, good and evil alike, nor of the reality and the violence of its battle with the latter. There is indeed a change as the centuries go by: the tenth-century *Canon Episcopi* of Bishop Regino of Prum sets out to uproot the arts of sorcery and malefice but also, at the same time, to uproot *belief* in the reality of night-riding and similar things which are in fact but phantasms imposed on the mind by the malignant spirit.[6] But as sorcery and witchcraft come to be more and more associated with heresy, the Church becomes more and more active in opposing them; by the fifteenth century the *Canon Episcopi* is held no longer to apply in its entirety because of the changed circumstances of the times, and it is in this century that Charles Williams sees the 'great war between Christendom and the devil' as opening: the century of the great trials, when King Henry V accused his stepmother of trying to murder him by magic arts, when Joan of Arc was accused of demon-worship, the Duchess of Gloucester was found guilty of magical practices, and, most famous and infamous of all, Gilles de Rais was tried and put to death for satanism and the mass-murder of children.[7]

The real frenzy and savagery were to come later. The fifteenth century still retains the medieval mixture, strange to so many modern minds, of coldly logical severity and Christian tenderness: Gilles de Rais was threatened with torture, and as his confession of enormities went on and on the presiding bishop rose and veiled the crucifix on the wall; but then, as the confession ended, the bishop came down to the prisoner and embraced him,

[6] cf. Williams, *op. cit.*, p. 73. [7] *ibid*, p. 101.

praying.[8] The story of this trial stands out in sharp contrast to that of the sufferings of Urban Grandier in the seventeenth century:[9] by then the temper had substantially changed, and the witch-hunting assumed monstrous proportions—Williams mentions five thousand burnings in Alsace alone between 1615 and 1635, and nine hundred in Bamberg between 1609 and 1633—and they remain monstrous even when one has given full weight to the testimonies as to the enormous prevalence of *maleficia*, to the general horror caused by such exposures as that of Gilles de Rais, and (to revert to our main concern here) to the conviction that these human enormities were inspired by the destructive will of a malevolent spirit of immense might and inexhaustible malignity. Yet the facts will not support the view that the whole of the war against Satan as it now raged can be written off as mass hysteria feeding upon uncritical credulity. The discussion as to whether human commerce with evil spirits is fact or delusion continued; the most famous of the medieval treatises, the *Malleus Maleficarum* of the Dominicans Sprenger and Kramer, by this time regarded as out of date, was replaced by such works as Bodin's *Discours des Sorciers* or Rémy's *Daemonolatreia*, in favour of belief in the material fact, and John Weyer's *De Prestigiis* and *De Lamiis*, which advocated a greater measure of scepticism and regarded witchcraft (as opposed to the great *arcana* of necromancy and the hermetic tradition) as belonging more to medicine than to theology.[10] By the middle of the seventeenth century

[8] cf. e.g. Williams, *op. cit.*, p. 122; D. B. Wyndham Lewis: *The Soul of Marshal Gilles de Raiz*, chapter 7.

[9] cf. A. Huxley: *The Devils of Loudun*, pp. 229–235.

[10] cf. Williams, *op. cit.*, pp. 206, 255, 260. The discussion is by no means dead, since modern Catholicism accepts both the possibility of diabolic possession and the findings of medical psychology; there was a case in recent years in the United States which was first diagnozed by several successive theologians in the former sense and then finally diagnozed by another—and successfully treated—in the latter.

the Roman Inquisition was calling for caution and de-
nouncing credulity; on the other hand in 1679 an arrest
in Paris for murder by poisoning led to the discovery of
magic practices which includes the black mass and child-
murder and involved Madame de Montespan and the
Abbé Guibourg.[11]

But the essential point is that, in all this controversy,
commerce with evil spirits, whether reality or phantasm,
was by general consent regarded as due to diabolic activity invading the material, human world in a horrible
travesty of the Incarnation and with the set intention of
setting at naught the effects of that Incarnation; and the
essential question is whether belief in at least the possibility of such an invasion is justified or not.

The eighteenth century, as might be expected, comes
down heavily on the side of scepticism. Addison believes
that such a thing as witchcraft exists but cannot credit
any particular instance of it;[12] the last death sentence
passed on a witch in England occurs in 1712 (and even
so the judge obtained the Queen's pardon for the condemned) and the Act of James I is repealed in the reign
of George II. Perhaps the nineteenth-century attitude is
summarized in a pitifully bland article in the ninth edition of the *Encyclopaedia Britannica* which declares:
'Educated public opinion has now risen above this level;
but popular credulity is still to be worked on by much
the same means as those employed by savage sorcerers
professing intercourse with familiar spirits.' So we come
to the supposition that the whole of the Christian (and
pre-Christian) tradition of belief in the existence, power
and activity of malignant spirits, of the 'principalities
and powers' of which St. Paul speaks, can be written off
in terms of a primitive anamism and of the power of suggestion working on superstition.

Nowadays we are less naive in our scepticism than was
the writer of the above article; yet undoubtedly the un-

---

[11] Williams, *op. cit.*, pp. 264 *sqq.*   [12] *ibid,* p. 301.

easiness, the reluctance to believe in any effective sense, remains. What conclusion then can we draw from analyzing the facts at our disposal?

As we have seen, the Church today accepts the reality both of diabolic possession and of the findings of modern psychopathology; it accepts also the extreme difficulty of distinguishing in practice between possession and mental disease—just as it accepts a similar difficulty where mystical and pseudo-mystical phenomena are concerned. The *Rituale* urges a reluctance (or, if the term be preferred, a healthy scepticism) in judging any given case as being one of true diabolic possession; on the other hand it includes the rite for the exorcism of evil spirits—and the rite of baptism itself includes the majestic banishing of Satan, in the name of the Omnipotent God, from the soul of the neophyte. Fr. Herbert Thurston, S.J., than whom no one could have been more 'healthily sceptical', wrote an article on 'spirits that bite' as being a question of fact. And historical facts do remain facts: the bones were found in the castle of Gilles de Rais; Grandier's at least alleged pact with the devil was discussed at his questioning;[13] the black mass indubitably was—and credibly still is—said; and if one contrasts the goodness, the 'decency', of the vast majority of human beings with the appalling burden of evil and horror which weighs down the world it is not easy to write off the 'mystery of iniquity' as a childish phantom.[14] We have indeed learnt a great deal from modern psychological research: no doubt a vast amount of what would once have passed for witchcraft and sorcery is explicable in terms of parapsychology or of the psycho-neuroses—or, where spiritist phenomena are concerned, of fraud. Yet the fact is that phenomena do occur which remain inexplicable or at least unexplained in natural terms. What

[13] cf. Huxley, *op. cit.*, p. 178.
[14] cf. my *The High Green Hill*, chapter xi, 'The Apostolate of Satan'.

for instance is a poltergeist? What are we to make of the satyrs of *Isaiah* or the Satan of *Job*? What is the 'mystery of iniquity'? What is the ultimate source and explanation, not just of human frailty, greed, animality, but of the cold intellectual malice, the love of evil and lust for evil for its own sake, superhuman rather than just subhuman in the sense of brutish, which are in fact to be found in man? Finally, what is the Christian to make of Christ's obvious acceptance of the reality both of Satan and of satanic possession?

But we must ask a further question: how could the worship and service of Satan *start*? The nineteenth century offered an answer as naive and smug as its view of witchcraft quoted above and as baseless as its bland assumption in the name of 'comparative religion', that the Christian mystery differs in no essential respect from the mystery-cults of the ancient world.[15] Primitive religions, it argued, involve belief in both gods and demons; obviously one tribe will regard as demons the gods of neighbouring hostile tribes; hence the psalmist's *omnes dii gentium daemonia*, 'all gods of the Gentiles are devils'—and all the Gentiles, in consequence, are devil-worshippers. This is all too facile. There is to say the least another possibility.

The question of idolatry is a complex one; insofar as idolaters set out to worship and obey a Supreme Being there is obviously something of good in what they do, no matter by what name they call him and even though their idea of him is a wild and perhaps savage distortion of the truth. On the other hand if Satan does exist, and exist as the Bible depicts him, he must be wholly opposed to the true worship of God, so that nothing is more likely than that he will turn all his resources to the task of utilizing pagan cults for his own evil ends—which may explain

[15] cf. Hugo Rahner, 'The Christian Mystery and the Pagan Mysteries', in *The Mysteries*, Eranos Yearbooks; also my *The Paradise Tree*, chapter 1.

why some of the cults contain such vile and evil elements. Again, the myths and rites of humanity express man's basic needs and yearnings, which is why they all follow the same essential pattern, but humanity is fallen, wounded in mind and will alike; and if, as some have thought, these myths and rites express in some sense a primitive God-given revelation we may expect to find distortions in them, so that again they will provide Satan with his opportunity. So it is that Milton treats pagan deities as being among the infernal powers, and his insight here would seem to be, if not pressed too far, a true one, consonant with the attitude of the Bible; for what those who preach the Gospel to idolaters are in effect saying is: You are trying to worship the Supreme Being and in so far as you do that you are 'in the truth'; but your picture of him is a false picture and therefore your god is a false god, and so we must try to show you the true picture and lead you to the true God.

But all that does not begin to explain the worship of the devil in a *Christian* society: Satan's existence and power are accepted, but why worship him since, for all his power, he is but a creature? James I in his *Demonologie* wrote that the answer was to be found in three passions: 'Curiosity in great ingines; thirst of revenge for some torts deeply apprehended: or greedy appetite of gear, caused through great poverty.'[16] Williams suggests that we should add to this list a fourth passion: 'the longings of sex and what other energies arouse variable phantasms in the human minds'[17]; we could mention too, as applicable at least to some moments in history, the cult of decadence, the *nostalgie de la boue,* and in general the fascination which evil as such can exercize over fallen human nature; and perhaps finally we should add a conscious and explicit hatred of God or more particularly of the divine humanity of Christ, arising from some unfathomable depth of despair or frustration or

[16] cf. Williams, *op. cit.,* p. 81.   [17] *ibid.*

wounded pride, and expressed in the blasphemies and obscenities of the black mass or the arrogant servility of the pact.

What, in Christian history, does the term 'satanism' in fact comprise? Traditionally at least some of the following elements are to be found: renunciation of the faith, expressed in blasphemy; allegiance to Satan, expressed in the explicit or implicit pact; the worship of Satan in the covens, the sabbats, the black mass; the serving of Satan's purposes through the *maleficium* and other forms of ill-doing; finally, sexuality and obscenity, the alleged commerce with incubi and succubi and the vilenesses of the sabbats.

Renunciation and allegiance figure in many stories and cannot be dismissed *a priori* from the domain of history. It is hard to take seriously most of the stories about familiar spirits, yet the use of animals in black magic and especially of animals fed on the Host in Satan-worship cannot simply be brushed aside, nor is there any doubt of the seriousness of the ruling in *Leviticus* that if a man or woman have a familiar spirit, 'dying let them die: they shall stone them'.[18] Even the night-riding, regarded as delusion by the *Canon Episcopi* and lending itself so readily to ridicule because of our mental image of the traditional witch astride her broomstick, does suggest interesting parallels with the phenomena of levitation in the hagiographies and with such oddities as the account of Home the medium flying through the window. But again the essential point is not whether night-ridings took place in fact or only in phantasm but that whatever did take place was attributed to the power of Satan.

The same applies to covens and sabbats: the stories describe assembly, dance, adoration, meal, orgy, plotting of evil; perhaps all this took place in fact; perhaps the witches really met but only the plotting was real (as the Berwick coven was reputed to have plotted against

[18] *Levit.* xx, 27 (Douai).

James I) and the rest phantasmal; perhaps the whole business took place only in dream: in any case the allegiance, the servitude, the love of evil remain the same.

Intercourse with incubi and succubi is regarded as matter of fact not only in the witch-trials but by theologians[19] and in a number of papal Bulls. What are we to think? The same principle holds: granting the existence of mighty, malignant spirits, it can be argued that their power would give them some control over matter perhaps to the point of achieving or simulating an act of coitus (there are details in the accounts, especially the emphasis on coldness—'cold as clay' said Rebecca West, the Essex witch, of her demon-lover's kiss[20]—which might be thought to have the ring of authenticity) but the essential facts remain unchanged if one argues instead that these things happened only in the imagination, perhaps the dream-life, of the people concerned. According to various testimonies some found the sexual congress pleasant, some painful, some agonizing; but the motivating factor in the demon's activity would be, not lust for fleshly pleasure, but something greater, deeper, more mysterious. Some Christian thinkers have seen the fall of the angels as due to a proud refusal to accept the divine plan of Incarnation; this would explain Satan's particular hatred of the divine Humanity, both in itself and in its eucharistic form. It would explain also the satanic attempt to travesty the Incarnation: in Hebrew legend the angelic Watchers lust after the daughters of men, and the myth (which either recurs as myth or is realized in fact in the aspect of satanism we are considering) shows a deep insight into Satan's designs in the world: because the Word was made flesh, flesh is immeasurably elevated and glorified, therefore flesh must be degraded; humanity was made glorious by a mysterious and wonderful union between human nature and

[19] cf. e.g. Liguori: *Praxis Confess.* VII, n.111; *Theol. Moral. lib.* III, *tract.* iv, c.2.　　[20] cf. Williams, *op. cit.*, p. 165.

Spirit, therefore it must be degraded by some sort of evil and grotesque parody; the divine act made humanity once again fruitful, productive, creative *in vitam aeternam*, therefore the satanic act must reduce and degrade humanity to doing only what is sterile, destructive. If we see satanism in this light we see it as precisely an attempted reversal of the Incarnation, and in so doing we can apprehend more of its scope, its magnitude, its malice. Some time ago a reviewer in one of the newspapers wrote of the black mass as 'childishness': perhaps it sometimes is, but we are wise to beware of facile generalizations. Even if we regard the accounts of the black mass in such writers as Huysmans as being mere 'literature', there are police reports which cannot be so lightly dismissed. It is not childishness to stab an infant in the throat and catch the blood in the chalice used at the mass; and though one may not believe in the Eucharist oneself, one can hardly regard as childish the profanation of the Host which in the eyes of millions of human beings is true God. The stringent regulations laid down, and from time to time re-emphasized, concerning the safety of the tabernacle on Catholic altars and the guarding of its key, are designed to prevent the theft and profanation not primarily of the sacred vessels but of their contents; and the periodical reminders are usually due to the recurrence of such thefts. To say that the black mass is always childish make-believe because dilettanti decadents sometimes dabble in what they like to think of as satanism is as silly as saying that the Mass is childish make-believe because some Catholics delight in *bondieuseries*.

There is then plenty of evidence which, if judged 'in a cool hour', can lead us to suppose that there is in fact active in the world an intellect of great might and malignity, a mystery of iniquity consumed with hatred of Christ and of his co-heirs and determined to attack the former by destroying the latter. There is plenty of evidence to lead us to suppose that the malignant power can and does attack humanity, an attack which is usually concerned with the corrupting and destroying of the soul but which also, because of the special hatred mentioned above, may involve direct attacks upon the body[21] and seek to destroy the soul through the corruption and degradation of the body. The Church, while holding that physical events and conditions may be due to supernatural causes good or evil, is well aware that exactly similar events and conditions may be purely self-induced; it is extremely difficult for instance to tell whether in the case of a stigmatic the undeniable, and undeniably bleeding, wounds in hands, feet and side are due to a real mystical experience or to a psychopathological condition. But in the case of events and conditions for which no reasonable explanation can be found from within the human personalities concerned, and which lead to other events and conditions beyond the normal range of human experience whether good or evil, it is reasonable to suppose that they are the result of eternal agencies greater than man. It may be well then to consider briefly what the Christian tradition has to tell us of such agencies.

The fourth Council of Lateran, in the early thirteenth century, was not saying anything new when it declared that God from the beginning of time had formed out of nothing two kinds of creature, the spiritual and the corporeal, the world of spirit and the world of earth; there is mention of these spirits all through the Bible from *Genesis* onwards. They are called angels, messengers, because it is as God's messengers that they intervene in human affairs as the story of man unfolds; so an angel was sent to Abraham to declare to him God's will and purposes, and, in the New Testament, to Mary to announce the Incarnation. They are sent as guardians and help-

[21] It is difficult to explain and still more to explain away, such occurrences as the beatings suffered by the Curé d'Ars : his own belief that they were satanic cannot be ruled out unless one has a better explanation to offer.

ers also; so Abraham tells his servant that the Lord 'will send his angel with thee to guide thee on thy journey',[22] and when the devil tempts Christ to throw himself down from the pinnacle of the temple he quotes to him the words of the psalmist that God 'hath given his angels charge over thee, and in their hands shall they bear thee up, lest perhaps thou dash thy foot against a stone'.[23] Our Lord speaks of angels (and, as we shall see later, of devils) in a matter of fact way that precludes mere metaphor: the 'legions of angels' whom he might summon to his aid, the angels who see the face of his Father, the angels at the judgement-day;[24] and belief in the existence of angels and in their power and their beneficent activity is constant throughout the Christian tradition from the earliest times.

This must be a question of belief, not of scientific proof; but at least we can show that the belief is reasonable, and this St. Thomas does, arguing from the idea of the *ordo universi*, the pattern of the created universe, and in particular from the idea of a measured hierarchy of created beings which leads one to suppose that the existence, at the lowest level, of sheer, inert matter will be balanced at the highest level by existences which are pure spirit. He goes on to argue that the angels are incomparably more in number than the species of material things,[25] and, drawing on the speculations of the pseudo-Denys, that they can be divided into three hierarchies according to the main differences of office or function—the contemplation of God, the governance of the world, the carrying out as messengers of God's behests.[26] They must be immortal because, being immaterial, pure spirit and therefore simple, they have within them no source of decomposition or dissolution.[27] They can be said to be in a given place only in the sense

---

[22] *Gen.* xxiv, 40.
[23] *Ps.* xc, 12.
[24] *Matt.* xxvi, 53; xviii, 10; xiii, 49.
[25] *Summa Theol.* I, l, 3.
[26] *ibid.* I, cviii, 9.
[27] *ibid.* I, 1, 5.

that their power is operative in it.[28] Finally, and most important to our present purposes, that power is very great; these are giant intellects, working in a way very different from and vastly superior to ours, since unlike us they have no need to abstract knowledge laboriously from sense-data, they are intuitive, and as even with us what we call a brilliantly intuitive mind can grasp instantly and at one glance what it will take a more plodding type of mind much labour to assimilate gradually, so also—but with an immeasurably greater swiftness, depth and sweep of vision—the angel-mind assimilates the reality presented to it in an instantaneous vision, and apprehends truth without any need of a rational discursus from premises to conclusion. All this is theirs of their nature; but there is, above and far beyond all this, their life of grace : they have the vision of God, and that vision includes an intuitive understanding of the mysteries of grace and of historical events as seen in the Word through whom all things are made. They are not of course omniscient; they cannot know the 'mysteries of God' of which St. Paul speaks, which are known only to the Spirit of God,[29] nor the secrets of men's hearts which according to St. Thomas are not part of the physical universe and are known only to God. But the depth and breadth, the sureness and piercing penetration of their knowledge are godlike indeed compared with ours, and are the measure of their greatness and their power.

These mighty spirits, the Christian tradition holds, were given some sort of initial probation, as were the first human beings; for God fashioned creatures endowed with intellect in order that they might love him, and to love means to love freely, to choose. Some did choose him, and therefore chose to adore and serve him; others refused, and turned away from him; and in turning away from God they turned away from life and light and condemned themselves to an unending search for

[28] *ibid.* I, lii, 1.   [29] *ibid.* I, lxiii, 7.

nothingness, disintegration, evil. Chief among them is the spirit we call Satan, Lucifer, the Adversary, whom many, including St. Thomas, think to have been the highest of all the angels; to him the Fathers apply the words which Isaiah wrote of the king of Babylon: 'How art thou fallen from heaven, O Lucifer, who didst rise in the morning? How art thou fallen to the earth, that didst wound the nations? And thou saidst in thy heart: I will ascend into heaven, I will exalt my throne above the stars of God . . . I will ascend above the height of the clouds, I will be like the most High.'[30] Satan is not the principle of evil, battling against God on equal terms, of the dualist religions; nor is he a mischievous but relatively harmless sprite. He is a creature, who, though fallen (by his own deliberate choice) from grace, is a mighty spirit still, his natural powers and qualities not destroyed but turned implacably to evil; terrifying yet beautiful still, a warped beauty, a brooding, icy malevolence.

There is only one reference to Satan (as a proper name, without the article) in the Old Testament; and though we identify with him other agencies such as the serpent in the garden of Eden, we learn little of his nature or history; he is simply an evil influence, concerned to induce man, as in the opening of the *Book of Job*, to rebel against God, whose 'angel' or—in some sense—emissary he is.[31] But as the Bible story unfolds, the references to him and to his activity become gradually clearer, more explicit. 'By the envy of the devil, death came into the world,' we read in the book of *Wisdom*;[32] and the *Apocalypse* describes how 'there was a great battle in heaven, Michael and his angels fought with the dragon, and the dragon fought and his angels: and they prevailed not, neither was their place found any more in heaven. And that great dragon was cast out, that old

[30] *Isaiah*, xiv, 12–14.　[31] cf. V. White, *op. cit.*, p. 177.
[32] *Wisd.* ii, 24.

serpent, who is called the devil and Satan, who seduceth the whole world; and he was cast unto the earth, and his angels were thrown down with him.'[33] And St. Peter writes of how the 'angels that sinned' were 'drawn down by infernal ropes to the lower hell, unto torments, to be reserved unto judgement'.[34] It is St. Peter, too, who warns us : 'Be sober and watch; because your adversary the devil as a roaring lion goeth about seeking whom he may devour';[35] the fall of man, man's repudiation of God, meant that the world was given over instead to the dominion of Satan. It was that dominion that Christ came to destroy, and did destroy, as he himself declared : 'Now shall the prince of this world be cast out'[36]—and when he speaks of having conquered the world[37] it is in that same sense of having dethroned Satan. Again, St. Paul speaks of our having been delivered from the power of darkness and translated into the kingdom of the Son ;[38] and we read in *Hebrews* of the Word being made flesh 'that through death he might destroy him who had the empire of death'.[39] And all this is applied to and made real in the individual soul in the rite of baptism, in which the priest commands the 'unclean spirit' to go forth from the neophyte and give place to the holy Spirit of God.

But if Satan's dominion is ended, his throne shattered, that does not mean that he is no longer active in the world. St. Peter's words have already reminded us that on the contrary he goes about like a raging lion. St. Paul warns us that 'our wrestling is not against flesh and blood but against principalities and powers, against the rulers of the world of this darkness, against the spirits of wickedness in high places';[40] though he adds elsewhere that God wll not allow us to be tempted beyond our strength.[41]

---

[33] *Apoc.* xii, 7–9.   [34] *II Peter*, ii, 4.   [35] *I Peter*, v, 8.
[36] *John*, xii, 31.   [37] *John*, xvi, 33.   [38] *Col.* i, 13.
[39] *Hebrews*, ii, 14.   [40] *Ephes.* vi, 12.   [41] *I Cor.* x, 13.

There are various ways in which Satan can continue to attack humanity. First, by temptation in the ordinary sense; he cannot, according to St. Thomas, influence the human will directly, but he can do so indirectly by appeals to the external senses or the imagination.[42] And if it is true that the diabolic intellect cannot err except with regard to supernatural realities,[43] we may suppose that the devil will be aware of the main proclivities to evil, the chief weaknesses, in each individual and will direct his attack accordingly.[44]

Secondly, there is the possibility of physical violence, already touched on with reference to the Curé d'Ars. Men long ago discovered that it was possible to break a man's spirit by breaking his body; it would be strange if the devil were less well informed about the implications of our psychophysical nature.

Thirdly, there is the possibility of diabolical possession. There is obviously no doubt in our Lord's mind as to the reality of this; he addresses the demons directly, sometimes silencing them, sometimes commanding them to speak, and the words of the priest in the baptismal rite are a repetition of those of Christ: 'Go out of the man, thou unclean spirit.'[45] It will be remembered that St. Mark goes on to tell us how our Lord asked, 'What is thy name?' and that the reply was, 'My name is Legion, for we are many.' In the early Church cases of diabolic possession seem to have been frequent, and the minor ecclesiastical order of exorcist was conferred to empower men to deal with them. Today, solemn and public exorcism is rare and requires episcopal authorization; but exorcism in private is permissible even to lay people, and its more frequent use encouraged by such theologians as Noldin and Prümmer.[46]

Fourthly there is the question of disease, physical and

42 *Summa Theol.* I, II, lxxx, 1 & 2.   43 cf. *ibid.* I, viii, 5.
44 cf. Vann & Meagher: *Stones or Bread?*   45 *Mark*, v, 8.
46 cf. V. White, *op. cit.*, pp. 186–7.

mental, in general. Our Lord makes it clear that disease is not necessarily the result of any sin on the part of the sufferer or of his parents; at the same time he speaks of the woman afflicted with curvature of the spine as having been 'bound' by Satan,[47] and Christianity teaches that the spiritual power of evil is in some way at the root not only of all human sin but also of its consequences, of pain and suffering and death. Certainly it seems unwarrantable to admit the reality of diabolic possession on the one hand and on the other to deny any connection at all between Satan and other mental and physical disorders. 'St. Thomas knows nothing of the facile distinction, which we find for instance in the *Catholic Encyclopaedia* and most latter-day Catholic literature, between mental disorder which comes from "natural causes" and mental disorder which comes from diabolic agency. For him, the devils can *only* act upon the human mind through natural, physical and psychological causes; and conversely all natural physical causes can be instruments of diabolic purposes. Truly enough, there are cases in which paranormal phenomena are more in evidence, but we seem to have no warrant at all for limiting diabolic agency and purpose to these.'[48]

Finally there is the question of activity resulting from the invocation of Satan by his worshippers, a diabolical travesty of the divine answer to prayer. The invitation need not be a direct and conscious one: the Church forbids spiritualist practices not because it denies the possibility of communicating with the dead but because the spiritualist *séance*, where it is not a fraud (as so many have been proven to be), is a dangerous dabbling in the unknown, dangerous precisely because if we lay the psyche open to influences from the other world we have no guarantee that it will not in fact be invaded by influences quite other than those we would have wished. But the invitation can be quite conscious: a deliberate calling down of the dark powers, a supplication to 'Our Father

[47] *Luke,* xiii, 11, 16.   [48] V. White, *op. cit.,* p. 185.

who wert in heaven'; and even if the supplication is a
childish game it is unlikely (if Satan is what Christianity
declares him to be) to end as a game.

Some modern investigators have seen the invocation of
Satan as not only real but widespread. Montague Summers asserted that satanism is in fact 'a vast and methodi-
cally regulated organization with cells and centres all
over the world . . . an international fifth column, which is
all energy and activity today'; and again that 'the cult of
the devil is the most terrible power at work in the world
today'.[49] We might compare with this the weightier authority of an encyclical of St. Pius X in 1903: 'So great,'
he wrote, 'is the general perversion that there is room to
fear that we are experiencing the foretaste and begin-
nings of the evils which are to come at the end of time,
and that the Son of Perdition, of whom the Apostle
speaks, has already arrived upon earth.' We have every
reason to think, with Berdyaev, that we are passing in
these present times not just through a crisis in human history but through the crisis of human history, the crisis of
humanity; and it is not difficult to see in the amassing of
the evils and horrors which weigh upon the world—the
wars, persecutions, tortures, enslavements, diseases of
body and mind, and, to crown all these, the constant fear
of mankind's total self-destruction—a sign of satanic activity more intensive than ever before and an echo of the
words with which Christ describes the fears and horrors
which would presage cosmic catastrophe.

True, we have to weigh carefully St. Paul's warning to
the Thessalonians against suggestions that 'the day of the
Lord is close at hand'.[50] The passage is obscure because
St. Paul breaks off; he has talked to them about all this
before by word of mouth, he reminds them. But certain
points are clear: before the second coming of the Lord
two other events must take place: first, the 'apostasy'
from the faith to which Christ himself had alluded when

[49] M. Summers: *Witchcraft and Demonology*, pp. 71, 223.
[50] II *Thess.* ii, 2 *sqq.*

he spoke of how false prophets would arise and seduce many, and of how the charity of many would grow cold;[51] secondly, the coming of Anti-christ, the 'man of sin' or 'champion of wickedness'[52] who will enthrone himself in the temple and proclaim himself as God. But for the time being, St. Paul continues, there is a power which holds evil in check and defers the coming of the Anti-christ until the appointed time, though it remains true that the 'mystery of iniquity' is already at work, doing secretly what the 'man of sin' will do openly.

The moral then seems to be a double one; we are not to neglect the ordinary business of living because of an unfounded conviction that the end of the world is upon us; on the other hand we are not to minimize the importance of the superhuman evil which is in our midst, or of that cunning which was stressed in the *Genesis* story and is stressed again by St. Paul.[53] Again, we are not to contribute to what has been called Satan's greatest triumph, his success in causing men to deny his existence; on the other hand we are not to make him a convenient scapegoat, 'projecting' all our sinfulness on to him so as to feel blameless ourselves.

But the final word must surely be the repudiation of fear. In the *Epistle of St. James* it is said of the devils that *credunt et contremescunt*, they believe that there is only one God—and 'shrink from him in terror';[54] for theirs is a dead, a loveless faith. We for our part, while having a wholesome fear of Satan's power, are not to let fear predominate, for the promise is given us that that power is doomed, and our Lord explicitly tells us not to be afraid: 'Fear not, I have conquered the world.' The power works secretly: it must be secretly undermined, by the quiet, constant efforts of loving Christians to fill the world with the power of love.

[51] *Matt.* xxiv, 11–12.
[52] So called in the Douai and Knox versions respectively.
[53] *Ephes.* vi, 11.   [54] *ibid.* ii, 19 (Knox).

Boethius, remote from us as he is in time, will none the less repay abundantly any care and study we can give him today, not only because of the beauty and profundity of his writings, but in particular because his personality and his thought have lessons for us which are specially relevant at the present time.

Like ourselves, he lived at the end of one world and the beginning of another; and to think of him, exiled and imprisoned for his faith, writing his most famous work in Theodoric's dungeon, and steeling himself against barbarous death by recourse to wisdom, to God, is inevitably to think of contemporary parallels. But also, the things he particularly stands for are things which we in our day particularly need.

The story of his life as we know it is quickly told. Anicius Manlius Torquatus Severinus Boethius was born about the year 470 of patrician family; he studied in Rome and in Athens; he then entered the service of the Ostrogoth king Theodoric, first as consul and then as *magister palatii*; thereafter he was accused of conspiracy and condemned by the king to exile and prison and finally executed at Pavia about 525. It was long held that his condemnation was a religious issue; that he was in fact a martyr to the Catholic faith; but this view was challenged when modern criticism questioned the authenticity of his theological treatises and refused to regard the *Consolation of Philosophy* as a proof of his Christianity. The controversy is now happily over: the discovery in 1877 of a fragment of Cassiodorus mentioning the treatise *De Trinitate* and other theological works of Boethius put the question of their authenticity beyond dispute; and in any case it is very difficult for an unbiassed mind to fail to see the Christianity in the *Consolation*. As M. Gilson remarks, he speaks as a philosopher but he thinks as a Christian.[1] And Dr. D. J. B. Hawkins has pointed out that Theodoric was tolerant of Catholicism so long as the eastern emperor was a monophysite, but that on the accession of the Catholic Justin I at Constantinople it was easy for the Gothic leaders to make the ageing Theodoric suspicious of his Catholic subjects; and the downfall of Boethius followed.[2] It is interesting, and consoling, to note that his cult as *beatus* at Pavia was confirmed by the Congregation of Rites in 1883.

That he had, then, before his downfall a rich, exalted, colourful life is evident; to discover his personality we have to go to his works. These reveal a fine mind, wise, deep, humane. Perhaps the best description of him is that given by Miss Helen Waddell in her *Wandering Scholars* : 'Not Augustine himself,' she writes, 'breaks his mind upon eternity as Boethius did'; and she points out that where Augustine in a mood of abnegation speaks of God in terms of a 'deep but dazzling darkness', Boethius sees rather 'a multitude of quiet stars'—his poems indeed seem to be studded with stars—and 'in Theodoric's dungeon, in presence of torture and imminence of death, the ex-senator steadies his soul on their unchanging way :

> *Look to the highest of the heights of heaven,*
> *See where the stars still keep their ancient peace.*

He is both mystic and stoic, but without the contempts of either; a lover of life and unafraid of death, but neither its shadow nor the light of the world to come has taken from the greenness of the grass. It was fortunate for the sanity of the Middle Ages that the man who taught them so much of their philosophy, whose book was "for the youngest in our schools", was of a temperament so humane and so serene; that the *maxime scrutator mag-*

---

[1] Gilson : *La Philosophie du Moyen Age*, 2nd edit. 1944, p. 146.
[2] Hawkins : *A Sketch of Medieval Philosophy*, p. 17.

narum rerum, "mightiest observer of mighty things", who defined eternity with an exulting plenitude that no man has approached before or since, had gone to gather violets in a spring wood, and watched with a sore heart a bird in a cage that had caught a glimpse of waving trees and now grieved its heart out, scattering its seed with small impotent claws.'[3]

His influence on the Middle Ages was immense. In the first place, Gilson speaks of him as the man who taught the Middle Ages logic until the whole Organon of Aristotle was translated :[4] he translated and commented on the *Isagoge* of Porphyrius, the *Categories, Analytics* and *Topics* of Aristotle; and he wrote further treatises of his own.

Secondly, he stated the problem which was to exercize so many minds, and cause such acrid disputes, throughout the Middle Ages : the problem of universals. Do genera and species exist in themselves ? It was this that gave rise to a certain amount of mockery of Boethius himself. Porphyrius in the *Isagoge* had stated the problem without offering a solution, since his immediate concern was with logic only; Boethius in his commentary on the *Analytics* gives the Aristotelean solution (*subsistunt ergo circa sensibilia, intelliguntur autem praeter corpora*), but gives Plato's view also; and it was this that gave rise to Godfrey of St. Victor's jingle :

> *Assidet Boethius, stupens de hac lite,*
> *Audiens quid hic et hic asserat perite,*
> *Et quid cui faveat non discernit rite,*
> *Nec praesumit solvere litem definite*

which one might perhaps translate—very roughly indeed—

> *Boethius is sitting there, marvelling at the shindy*
> *Raging either side of him, erudite and windy,*
> *Not seeing as between the two just which of them is right,*
> *Nor venturing himself to give an answer definite.*

[3] Waddell, *op. cit.,* pp. xxvi–xxvii.   [4] Gilson, *op. cit.,* p. 139.

But in point of fact his own view is given in the *Consolation*, Book V, where, describing how 'sense, imagination, reason and understanding do diversely behold a man', he says of the understanding that, 'surpassing the compass of the whole world, it beholdeth with the clear eye of the mind that simple form in itself'—the Platonic Idea; and again, in the *De Trinitate*, II, he writes : 'We misname the entities that reside in bodies when we call them forms; they are mere images; they only resemble those forms which are not incorporate in matter.'

It had indeed been Boethius' aim to translate and comment upon the whole work of Plato and Aristotle and to show their fundamental accord. He fell very short of achieving this immense purpose, but he left, among other things, a grand definition of philosophy and a classification of the various disciplines which it includes and governs. He coined the phrases Quadrivium, the fourfold way to wisdom (arithmetic, astronomy, geometry, music) and Trivium, the threefold mode of expressing knowledge (grammar, rhetoric, logic) ; and his treatises on music, arithmetic and geometry were, according to Gilson, practically all that the Middle Ages had on these subjects for a very long time.

In one of the theological treatises Boethius states the problem which St. Thomas was finally to meet and solve : *fidem si poterit rationemque coniunge* : 'to reconcile if possible faith and reason';[5] and his importance for St. Thomas may be gauged, for instance, by the fact that the latter wrote an important commentary on his treatise *De Trinitate*, and adopted his definitions of person (*naturae rationalis individua substantia*), of beatitude (*status omnium bonorum congregatione perfectus* : that state which is perfect in the aggregation of all good things), and, most famous of all, the lapidary definition of eternity which

---

[5] *Utrum Pater et Filius et Spiritus Sanctus de Divinitate substantialiter praedicentur.*

echoes and re-echoes through the centuries : *interminabilis vitae tota simul et perfecta possessio* : 'the perfect and simultaneous possession of endless life'. He also, incidentally, supplied St. Anselm with another famous definition of God, as that *quo melius nihil cogitari queat* : 'than which nothing more perfect can be conceived'.

But Boethius' greatest single contribution to the thought of the Middle Ages and indeed to the culture of the west as a whole is of course the *Consolation of Philosophy*. In this book he gave the medieval thinkers an example of a Christian work of pure philosophy; but he gave them much more than that; and it is here especially that what he has to offer seems so apt to our present condition and needs.

In the first place, Boethius is a humanist in the best sense of the term : a lover of beauty and wisdom and all that we mean by the humanities. The beauty of his own language proves it; and in his verse especially (the *Consolation* is composed of five books of alternating prose and verse passages) he is always returning to the beauty of the earth and the skies :

>   *tu cuncta superno*
> *Ducis ab exemplo, pulchrum pulcherrimus ipse*
> *Mundum mente gerens similique in imagine formans*
> *Perfecta iubens perfectum absolvere partes*

> *Thy goodness moving thee to give each thing his grace,*
> *Thou dost all creatures' forms from highest patterns take;*
> *From thy fair mind the world fair like thyself doth make,*
> *Thus thou perfect the whole perfect each part doth*
>   *frame.*[6]

He is no stranger to the *lacrimae rerum*, the tears which lie at the heart of things : the glittering of beauty, he says, is but *velox et vernalium florum mutabilitate fugacior* : 'as suddenly decaying and changing as the frail

---

[6] *Cons.* III, 9. The translations here given are from the 'I.T.' version in the Loeb edition.

flowers in the spring.'[7] He has something of the Greek exaltation of friendship: *pretiosissimum divitiarum genus*, he calls it, 'the most precious treasure in the world', and again, *sanctissimum genus*, 'that most sacred thing'; and he attributes it rather to virtue than to fortune;[8] and it is interesting to speculate whether the medieval attitude to *amicitia*, often presented as in Greece as the supreme form of love, is not in its turn due largely to his influence. The famous phrase, *in omni adversitate fortunae infelicissimum est genus infortunii fuisse felicem*, 'in all adversity of fortune it is the most unhappy kind of misfortune to have been happy', immediately inspired Dante's *nessun maggior dolore che ricordarsi del tempo felice nella miseria*.[9] His humanity is constantly apparent; and has its quiet touches of humour, as when he describes men whose minds, though obscured, yet seek after the greatest good, but *velut ebrius domum quo tramite revertatur ignorat*, 'like a drunken man know not the way home'. In beauty, warmth and dignity of style and doctrine alike, then, he is at the farthest possible remove from the dry academic scholasticism, the dusty logic-chopping, into which Christian thought sometimes in the Middle Ages degenerated and still, alas, degenerates.

But if his humanism is a very apt reminder of human richness and dignity in a world which is doing its best to destroy the humanities, his definition of philosophy and his attitude towards it make him still more valuable as a corrective at the present time. For Boethius, philosophy is the love of wisdom, but of wisdom as a reality, that 'living thought which is the cause of all, and which is self-subsistent, God'; and which, illuminating the mind of man, draws him to itself by love.

In other words, his attitude to truth is the exact opposite of a view largely and disastrously prevalent today. We live in a world in which the accent, here as elsewhere,

[7] III, 8.   [8] II, 8; III, 2.   [9] II, 4.

is all on the idea of possession, mastery, domination, power, activism. Just as life is thought of in terms of possessing power or wealth or pleasure or influence, and love is thought of as possessing something or somebody, so knowledge is thought of as possessing truth, and using the truth possessed so as to master nature, to acquire power. All this is the fruit of an excessive emphasis on practical scientific reason and indeed of its exaltation to the rank of supreme exercize of intellect; and it has robbed our world of vision, and therefore of wisdom, and in the last resort of life. There is far more knowledge in the world today than ever before; and, it would seem, far less wisdom. Almost all the wisdom which humanity has learnt intuitively through the ages is now lost to us. And the moral is, that the first thing we have to do is to relearn the lesson that for human beings, male and female alike, the essential condition for becoming wise is first to be feminine to reality : to see life as being possessed *by* life, the mind and heart open to reality, letting reality flood in; to see love as being possessed *by* love, living in love; to see wisdom as being possessed *by* the truth; to see holiness in terms not first of action but of passion, of experiencing divine things.

Professor Guitton has suggested that we are perhaps approaching an 'age of Mary', in which the influence of the mother of God will assume new proportions;[10] and it is interesting to link this view with two other readings of human history, as put forward, for example, by Berdyaev on the one hand and by Mr. E. I. Watkin on the other. The former, in his book on Dostoievsky, writes of the age of Dante, which worships a transcendent God and accepts therefore a cosmic order from without; a second age, of Shakespeare, the Renaissance, which dethrones the transcendent God and his order, his heaven and hell, and worships the purely immanent god of humanity; and then finally a third age, in which the dark realities of the

[10] cf. *The Blessed Virgin*, p. 180.

underworld which the preceding age had ignored refuse
to be ignored any longer and burst forth, and God is
found again, not now merely as transcendent in his
heaven—still less of course as the purely immanent
pseudo-god—but both transcendent and immanent, the
transcendent but *redemptive* God, revealed therefore as
immanent *in* the squalors of humanity, the dark waters,
out of which he will bring new light and new life through
sharing in them, as in the beginning he brought light and
life out of the dark waters of chaos.

The third view, as represented by Mr. E. I. Watkin,
modifies the theory of the medieval abbot Joachim of
Flora which saw history in terms of three ages, of Father,
Son and Holy Spirit respectively. The third age, in this
modern presentation of the theory, does not supersede
the age of the Son : it completes it, as Pentecost com-
pleted the Passion : it signifies that, within the reign and
rule of the Word over the world, there is to come a time
when the influence of the Paraclete will be more intense
than before : when Christianity—love of God, obedience
to God—will become more and more *inward* : a contemplative age, therefore, dominated more and more completely by the inward motivations of charity and the
Gifts : an age of the Spirit.

Now symbolically all these three things, the Mother,
the Waters, the Spirit, are very closely linked; and they
all express that basic attitude which is so lacking today,
and without the recovery of which there can be no hope
for our survival as a civilization. The mother, the waters,
the spirit : to be feminine to reality and so learn wisdom :
to be moulded by reality and so achieve fullness; to rest
in reality and so achieve peace : these are the essential
lessons we have to learn, and it is here that Boethius and
his attitude to philosophy are so valuable for us.

It was his own personal ambition, when holding high
office, to enact the Platonist idea of the philosopher-king :
to make sure that power should be put to the service of
wisdom, not of shortsighted knowledge or of folly. And

the Philosophy who consoles him in his dungeon is a woman; she leads him to Wisdom (*Sophia, Sapientia, Sagesse*); she is the *summum lassorum solamen animo-rum,* the most effectual refreshment of wearied minds; if, she tells him, he had not cast away the weapons she had given him he would have been invincible against the attacks of evil fortune; but she leads him gently back to the realization that not in the gaining possession of anything but only in the love of and obedience to God's will is there any hope of happiness. When you are possessed *by* life and *by* peace, then you are fully alive and your peace is unbreakable.

'Every sudden change of things,' she tells him, 'happeneth not without a certain wavering and disquietness of mind';[11] but at the same time there would be peace of soul for us if only we did not seek for our felicity abroad whereas it is placed within ourselves. 'If thou settest up thy sails to the wind,' she says again, 'thou shalt be carried, not whither thy will desirest, but whither the gale driveth.'[12] 'Have you no proper and inward good,' she asks, 'that you seek your goods in those things which are outward and separated from you?' *O praeclara opum mortalium beatitudo, quam cum adeptus securus esse desistis*: 'O excellent happiness of mortal riches (external things) which when thou hast gotten thou hast lost thy safety!'[13]

Inwardness: it is here again that Boethius sounds a note that we in these days need desperately to hear and understand. God is the still point at the centre of the wheel; the further you move from that point towards the circumference, the more you lose your freedom and become the plaything of fortune; the more you cleave to God and love his providence, the greater your freedom and therefore your happiness; it is then that you can say, as Philosophy does say in stoic vein, *Nec speres aliquid, nec extimescas*: 'For nothing hope, nor fear thou harm'; though indeed in its total context it is less a statement of

[11] II, 1.　　[12] *ibid.*　　[13] II, 5.

pagan stoicism than of a Christian understanding of the *nunc stans*: that quiet, tranquil living in the present which is also a living in the Presence, in the unsleeping and unwavering care of God.

A Christian understanding of the *nunc stans*, but also, it should be added, of humility. God created man, Boethius writes in the *De Fide Catholica*, that as the higher (angelic) nature had fallen low through the curse of pride, so the lower substance might ascend on high through the blessing of humility. It is this same humility which is one of the conditions of tranquillity :

> *Humili domum memento*
> *Certus figere saxo—*

> . . . *thy poor house bestow*
> *In stony places firm and low.*
> *For though the winds do sound*
> *And waves of troubled seas confound:*
> *Yet thou to rest disposed*
> *In thy safe lowly vale inclosed,*
> *Mayst live a quiet age,*
> *Scorning the air's distempered rage.*[14]

It is again, incidentally, Boethius' grasp of the meaning of eternity which enables him to find a solution to the problem of the compatibility of human free will with the divine fore-knowledge of future contingents. This he treats in the fifth book of the *Consolation*. If divine prevision, he argues, is infallible, then we cannot act otherwise than in accord with it, and so are not free; if on the other hand we do have freedom of choice, then God's prevision cannot be infallible. Boethius proceeds to offer a solution to the problem in terms of a distinction between what is infallibly foreseen and what is necessary : a distinction of which St. Thomas will make use. Human free acts are indeed foreseen, but foreseen precisely as free (St. Thomas will say that God wills both the event and the free mode of the event); and Boethius

---

[14] II, 4.

shows how this can be precisely by invoking the nature of eternity. We ought not, strictly, to speak of God's *fore*-knowledge, for he sees everything simultaneously in the eternal present—for which reason we speak rightly of his providence, not of his previence; so that we must judge of his knowledge of what to us are future events as we judge of our own knowledge of events actually taking place before our eyes. The fact that I see a man walking does not mean that it is necessary for the man to walk.

But to return : to think of the mother, the spirit, the water, *is* to think of inwardness : the Mother kept all these words in her heart; the Spirit is the indwelling Spirit who instructs the hearts of men; the waters lap you about, the waters of death, but become within you the waters of life, springing up into life everlasting. In one of Boethius' most majestic poems, which incidentally is a masterly summary of the *Timaeus* of Plato, he has a magnificent prayer :

Da pater augustam menti conscendere sedem
Da fontem lustrare boni, da luce reperta
In te conspicuos animi defigere visus—

Dear Father, let my mind thy hallowed seat ascend,
Let me behold the spring of grace and find thy light,
That I on thee may fix my soul's well-clearèd sight;

and a few lines later, the magnificent ending of the poem with its glorious string of nouns in the last line :

. . . Tu namque serenum,
Tu requies tranquilla piis, te cernere finis,
Principium, vector, dux, semita, terminus idem—

. . . Thou only calm and rest
To pious men whose end is to behold thy ray,
Who their beginning art, their guide, their bound, and way.[15]

Boethius speaks of the divine mind *in suae simplicitatis arce composita*: 'placed in the castle of its own simplic-

[15] III, 9.

ity';[16] and it is this simplicity of God which is the clue to
his treatment both of the supernal tranquillity and serenity of God, and at the same time of the tranquil serenity of
man in whom wisdom and goodness reign. For human
beatitude, Boethius is not afraid to say, consists in the
obtaining of divinity : *omnis igitur beatus deus*, each of
the blessed is God, not by nature but by participation;[17]
and to share divinity is to share also the stillness of
divinity, to find the still point in the flux of fate, and to
find happiness because highest freedom in willing and
loving what God wills and loves :

> *O felix hominum genus*
> *Si vestros animos amor*
> *Quo caelum regitur regat—*

> *How happy mortals were,*
> *If that pure love did guide their minds, which*
> *heavenly spheres doth guide!*[18]

Inwardness : wisdom means being possessed by the
truth which is God; happiness means living in and being
possessed by the joy which is God, the inward fruit of
which is that peace which the world cannot give and
cannot take away. This lesson Boethius reinforces by his
teaching concerning rewards and punishments; these too
are not something arbitrarily bestowed or inflicted from
without but simply the logical fulfilment of an inner
process : 'the reward of good men, which no time can
waste, no man's power diminish, no man's wickedness
obscure, is to become gods';[19] whereas 'he that, leaving
virtue, ceaseth to be a man, since he cannot be partaker
of the divine condition, is turned into a beast';[20] and so
it is that, in the end, even adversity is for the good man a
blessing : 'Wherefore, quoth she, a wise man must no
more be troubled when he is assaulted with adversity,

[16] IV, 6. [17] III, 10.
[18] II, 8. [19] IV, 3.
[20] *ibid.*

than a valiant captain dismayed at the sound of an alarum. For difficulties are the matter by which the one must extend his glory, and the other increase his wisdom.'[21]

We today do indeed seem to be living in the flux of fate; and we might well have recourse to Boethius to steady us. We live in a world which has largely lost its faculty of wonder, its power of natural contemplation. We have our poets but few will read them, our artists but few have interest in them, there are still the beauties and glories of Nature but few have time for them. We might well have recourse to Boethius to renew our wonder and love and understanding of the earth and its fullness and the beauty that comes forth from man's hand. We live in a world of restlessness and rootlessness, neurosis and fear; and we could do worse than pray sometimes the prayer of Boethius, *O stelliferi conditor orbis*, 'Creator of the star-decked skies':

O iam miseras respice terras
Quisquis rerum foedera nectis.
Operis tanti pars non vilis
Homines quatimur fortunae salo.
Rapidos rector comprime fluctus
Et quo caelum regis immensum
Firma stabiles foedere terras—

   O thou that joinest with love
All worldly things, look from thy seat above
   On the earth's wretched state;
We men, not the least work thou didst create,
   With fortune's blasts do shake;
Thou careful ruler, these fierce tempests slake,
   And for the earth provide
Those laws by which thou heaven in peace dost guide.[22]

[21] IV, 7.   [22] I, 5.

CARMELITE MONASTERY
Beckley Hill
Barre, Vt., 05641

BORROWED